Bob Kaplan MD and Gerard LeMoine

Desert PAWNS

Breaking The Cycle Of Reincarceration

PASSLINE PRODUCTIONS
SCOTTSDALE, ARIZONA

ISBN: 1450526063
ISBN-13: 9781450526067
Library of Congress Control Number: 2010900730

To Our Families

CONTENTS

PROLOGUE

The Topaz Correctional Facility (TCF), a concrete, two-story, razor-wire rimmed prison lying deep in the heart of the desert Southwest, was built in 1998 by Advanced Inmate Incarceration (AII), one of America's largest private prison corporations. The 2,300 bed medium-maximum security prison houses murderers, armed robbers, rapists and drug dealers, as well as some white collar criminals, and a few cannibals.

Why should you care? The 2.3 million inmates housed in America's prisons cost US taxpayers $60 billion annually! Since 80% of these individuals will eventually be paroled, whom do you want released from prison, an unskilled, violent predator, or an educated, job-ready individual committed to staying out of prison?

In the mid 1980s, the private-prison industry rose like a Phoenix from the ashes, fueled by Wall Street venture capitalists and the "Get Tough On Crime" mentality. Subsequent legislation, including mandatory minimum sentencing and the Three Strikes program frequently pushed by prison industry lobbyists, assured a steady stream of new inmates to fill the explosive construction of new facilities.

In the past two decades, America's prison population has quadrupled! During the same period, state spending on corrections facilities increased 127 percent, while education spending rose only 21 percent.

Akin to the decades-old military-industrial complex, a new prison-government complex emerged, with a cadre of well-connected players sitting on their boards, everyone from former governors and intelligence honchos, to retired generals.

The solution espoused by the prison industry seemed plausible: bring the efficiencies of the private sector to bear on America's burgeoning prison population. Instead of using taxpayer funds to build and staff corrections facilities, these costs were assumed by private firms, in exchange for lucrative contracts with state and federal agencies, Immigration and Customs Enforcement (ICE), and the US Marshals, as well as housing county and transit prisoners. More recently, they've expanded into management of INS facilities, juvenile detention centers and drug-treatment facilities. States with budgetary constraints house inmates at less cost in private prisons, accounting for the transfer of thousands of California inmates to corporate facilities in other states.

What began as an attempt to cut costs and provide more humane treatment produced unintended consequences. The advent of private prisons has created a *disincentive* to rehabilitate inmates! With corporate profits dependent on high occupancy rates, prisoners successfully reintegrated into society no longer occupy beds at the corporation's facilities and profits tank. Corrections Officers (COs) are laid off. Within private prison facilities, education and job training aren't viewed as cost-effective.

Think this view is unfair? Biased? What if it *were* possible to educate inmates at no additional corporate cost?

Working in conjunction with a dedicated group of volunteer outside educators, a courageous teacher at TCF named Gerard LeMoine instituted a rigorous educational program.

Using discipline and tough love, LeMoine transformed a group of hardcore offenders, effecting profound changes in their lives, by encouraging them to embrace education.

At the height of the program, over 1200 inmates requested educational courses. More inmates passed their GEDs (high-school equivalency tests) then at any time in the six years that the program had been operating. Under LeMoine's direction, a core group of eighty-four predominantly violent offenders published a collection of inmate writings, *Voices From The Desert.* During this period, violence among participants dropped precipitously. Inmates took a renewed interest in their appearance. Self-esteem soared. The program was so successful there was talk of expanding it to the corporation's satellite facilities.

Then, administration abruptly shut the program down.

This is the story of those events. Forget the hype you've read about prison education. After reading this book, you'll understand what's *really* happening within the system. Moreover, the techniques implemented by LeMoine provide a template for reforming education throughout the prison system.

"MEET YOUR NEW CELLIE"

Danny Whitecloud, aka Danielle, a flamboyant, forty-year-old Native American (NA) transvestite, was well known to COs at TCF. Just hours after being assigned a new cellie (cellmate), Danny, drenched in blood, walked out of his cell, tossing the cellie's severed head down the hallway. Turns out COs had given Whitecloud–who'd been molested as a child–a cellie who was a known sex offender! Was bunking them together simply an administrative oversight?

Federal guidelines mandate a preliminary background check on each inmate to determine suitability for housing. Each state's contract monitor is responsible for overseeing such details.

Under ordinary circumstances, incoming inmates are processed and assigned to one of three units: population (general population), PC (protective custody) or SEG (segregation). Inmates tagged as maximum-security automatically go to SEG for up to ninety days to get the message: The prison won't tolerate any shit.

Medium-security inmates are assigned to population or PC, a step down from SEG. Child molesters and snitches are assigned to PC for their own protection and are distinguished from other inmates by their orange jumpsuits.

PC inmates are transported separately from the general population. During transport of PC inmates, other inmates in the hallway must turn away, their faces touching the wall. If they don't comply, one of the COs yelling, "Face the wall," forcefully pushes their head against the wall. Windows in the PC pods (housing units) are blacked out, precluding monitoring by other inmates.

Every new inmate gets a folder for personal papers, including arrest records, which they store in the footlocker in their cell. The first chance available, other inmates within the pod approach the new guy.

"Where're your papers?"

Danny Whitecloud's cellie was put there for the amusement of the COs. Whitecloud, serving time for murder, comes up for parole review every five years and is known to commit violent acts to stay within the institution. COs used the incident to intimidate other inmates.

"Step out of line, we'll put you in the cell with Whitecloud."

Kill someone in an orange jumpsuit, you're a hero. Rewards for killing a child molester include drugs, cigarettes, juice and cupcakes. Food is a big thing in prison.

The infirmary, education, administration, library, security, classrooms and half the SEG cells are on the first floor. The remainder of the facility is comprised of the pods, consisting of twenty two-man cells, ten cells on the top deck, ten below.

Each seven-by-twelve foot cell has a stainless steel sink and toilet. The fiberglass and stainless steel racks comprising the bunk beds reside within the back of the cell, next to the slit window, a six-inch by five-foot-tall, one-inch thick shatterproof pane of glass reinforced with chicken wire.

In a footlocker stowed beneath the bottom bunk, inmates store towels, underwear, books and nick knacks. There's a shelf, a gym locker and a small area on the wall for personal photos. Photos put up in unauthorized places are fair game for the COs, who tear them down as punishment for infractions.

Guys in for more than twenty years usually get their own cell–they're generally considered too edgy to bunk with others.

Multigenerational inmates—e.g., a grandfather, father and son (particularly Hawaiians and Alaskans) bunk in the same pod.

Electrical outlets in the cells accommodate TV's, headsets and Gameboys, utilized by staff to pacify inmates.

"Go in your cell. Play games. Shut up."

These items, in addition to such things as tennis shoes and compass-less watches, must be purchased through the prison commissary at inflated prices. TVs have clear plastic housing to facilitate inspection. Cable TV costs extra. Inmates cherish their tennis shoes. Steal someone's tennis shoes and you could pay with your life.

When released from their cells, prisoners congregate in a common area within the pod centered around bolted down, laminated picnic tables and two TVs suspended eight feet up the wall and bolted down on two heavy-duty steel shelves. Meals are served in the central hallways, cafeteria-style, then taken back to the pods to be eaten. Meals are rarely served on time.

For an hour a day, inmates are released into the exercise yard, where they have access to weight stations or can play basketball. The facility replaces two to three basketballs a week, chewed up on the razor wire rimming the perimeter fence.

The entire prison, including classrooms and hallways, is wired for sound. Consequently, staff members discussing sensitive issues walk out to the parking lot or talk over lunch at a nearby restaurant. Speakers within the cells allow COs to eavesdrop on conversations.

"Who's got the tattoo gun?"

One would think inmates would cover the speakers, but they frequently forget.

Inmates are monitored by closed-circuit TV, utilized by administration to cover chronic staff shortages.

Throughout the prison, air-conditioning is spotty. Classrooms and administration are always hot, while most pods are so cold inmates block the vents, shoving wadded-up pieces of toilet paper into the small ceiling vents. COs punish bad behavior by sticking Alaskans in the hot pods. Hawaiians caught acting out face sudden transfer to a frigid pod.

"OK, grab your shit!"

Water within the facility is undrinkable. Drinking fountains throughout TCF are shut off. The sight of a staff member racing to the bathroom is not uncommon. At one point, diarrhea was so rampant that the prison ran out of toilet paper. Anti-diarrheal meds dispensed by the infirmary are frequently outdated. Seasoned staff carry bottled water.

How do the inmates survive? Traditional holidays double as fund-raisers to pay for Brita filters and pitchers purchased at full price from the commissary. Vets' groups use the Fourth of July and Veteran's Day. Faith pods collect money during Easter. Alaskans hold potlucks (potlatches). Hawaiians raise funds during Asian New Year, while the Black Muslims raise money prior to Ramadan and during Black History month.

Lifers, those who've found Jesus, and inmates awaiting release inhabit the faith pod. Some of these men would likely be assaulted if placed within the general population. Afternoon Bible classes are held within these pods, which have a reputation for running a specific form of contraband.

Undocumented illegals held under contract with ICE are housed in three twenty-by- forty-foot cells atop the pods, in a separate wing. Up to fifty guys cram into each cell and sleep in shifts on mattresses on the floor. One group sleeps, while the others sit out in the common area of the pod watching TV. Soccer is a favorite.

Entrance to the ICE holding cells is through three secured doors. Once inside, the stagnant, humid air yields the gut-wrenching aroma of sweat admixed with excrement, partially masked by the stench of cheap bleach.

The mantra among the COs is "shove 'em in and process 'em." Undocumented illegals are told to strip and are issued jumpsuits. They aren't always showered.

The AC to these holding cells often malfunctions. The two toilets within each cell frequently overflow. Prisoners often urinate or defecate in buckets placed within cells for cleanup. Many inmates housed at the facility have to be taught to use toilets and toilet paper. Among prisoners, especially illegals, infectious diseases are rampant, particularly hepatitis and malaria. *E. coli* outbreaks are not uncommon. Several inmate deaths caused by *staph* infections were officially attributed to other causes. Health and safety inspectors frequently bypass the ICE holding cells because they're "too contagious."

Segregation is utilized for inmates who are violent, crazy or face punishment for specific offenses. Uncontrollable or aggressive SEG inmates are regarded as good training material for the prison's Special Operations and Response Team (SORT) team. Crazy inmates are readily turned in by others.

"This guy's crazy. Get him the fuck out of here!"

Throughout the facility, the COs do a head-count every two hours. It's always off.

IF YOU'RE ASIAN, YOU'RE A MEMBER

The walls along the facility's walkways are adorned with ornate murals. Painstakingly created by inmates utilizing acrylic applied to the cement block wall, these scenes are a source of pride and evoke memories of home – elk running through the Alaskan wilderness, dolphins swimming in the Pacific. Other murals depict life-size images of the Dallas Cowboys.

Alongside these scenes, are AII's ever-present mission statements.

"Treat our clients as you want to be treated."

Who are their clients?

A number of "associations" operate within the facility. The term "gang" is not allowed. The largest, the USO (United Samoan Organization), runs the prison.

Never heard of them? They comprise all Pacific Rim gang members from New Zealand to Japan, including Hawaiians, Samoans, Japanese, Thai, Burmese, Malay, Indonesians, Yap, Truk and Solomon Islanders. If you're Asian, you'd better be a member.

For years, Hawaiian prisons operated by a different code than their counterparts on the mainland. A dispute between an inmate and CO was settled outside in the prison exercise yard, one on one. No one interfered. If a prisoner called a guard out, he had to go. Once the fight was over, the matter was closed. Since 1995, prison overcrowding and the high cost of available land propelled the state of Hawaii to ship inmates to private prisons within the continental US.

The USO are very polite, open, honest. As part of their code, they'll admit wrongdoing. Unlike other inmates, the Hawaiians rarely lie; they'll evade questions so they're not forced to be dishonest. At TCF, Hawaiian inmates and COs address each other as "Sir." The Hawaiians are uninterested in education.

"We're not here to take the white man's classes."

Hawaiian pods are immaculate. Marine clean. White-glove clean. They scrub everything from the toilets to the cracks in the tile. While reflexively opposed to inmate expenditures, TCF always approves requests by the Hawaiians for cleaning supplies.

"You want Lysol? You got it!"

To Hawaiians, family is paramount. Within the Hawaiian pod, if a CO tears down pictures of a family member, they're in a world of hurt.

Inmate's uniforms are essentially hospital scrubs, tie-off pants and a V-neck shirt. The Hawaiians wear tan uniforms, pressed by laying the clothes beneath the mattresses.

Hawaiian inmates are characteristically muscular and toned, with either a short hair cut (military style) or long hair worn in a ponytail.

Rice and pork are mainstays of the Hawaiian diet. Any attempt to disrupt their customs, for purposes of administrative punishment, evokes a violent response. In September 2000, the withholding of rice from Hawaiian inmates led to a rampage, during which a CO was assaulted— literally hung up in the air by torn sheets.

A tight-knit group within the facility, NA Alaskans are commonly imprisoned for alcohol-related homicides. Most posses a third-to-fifth grade education. Back home, they earn a living off the land as rural fishermen and seal hunters. Within the remote villages, incest and sodomy are reportedly rampant. Not surprisingly, heavy alcohol consumption among teens is commonplace, as are learning disabilities. Many inmates take more than a decade to obtain a GED.

The Alaska Permanent Fund manages revenues from the Trans-Alaska Pipeline System. Since 1982, the fund has dispersed yearly dividends to Alaskans living in the state a minimum of twelve months but specifically denies payment to white Alaskans serving time in prison.

Incarcerated NA Alaskans continue receiving royalties as tribal members from natural resource development—e.g. oil and precious metals, on native lands. These funds, which can amount to hundreds of thousands of dollars, are held by TCF in personal accounts for each inmate.

While gang participation among the Hispanics isn't mandatory, the majority of Hispanic inmates from Alaska and Washington State are gang members. Other well-known gangs include the Crips and the Bloods (two rival, predominantly African American gangs) originally founded in LA, the Muslim Brotherhood, the Skinheads and the Hells Angels. Participation in a gang sometimes reflects shared beliefs but often is about protection, the ability to obtain food or drugs or simply the chance to break the boredom of prison life.

Inmate-Satanists from Washington State and Alaska outright sacrificed virgins in the woods. The "purer" of these venerate Satan as a supernatural diety. Once a week (twice a month for evening mass) a female visitor meets with Satanists in the prison library/religious room. Robed in black, this High Priestess discusses such topics as sacrifices and summoning those in the underworld to do bidding. Inmates chant to the devil by candlelight.

Wiccans, practioners of white magic, also convene within the facility.

To prevent bloodshed, rival gangs are housed in separate pods. Within TCF, the corporation maintains state contracts for the imprisonment of inmates from California, Hawaii, Alaska, and Washington. Among gang members, allegiance is to race first, then state contract, i.e., when Hispanics face off against blacks, it doesn't matter what state they're from.

Conversely, while COs normally keep the races separated, Muslims can be black, white or Hispanic and are permitted to mix for religious services. Prison personnel are afraid of lawsuits and actively avoid creating the potential for litigation.

Observance of Ramadan is an opportunity for Muslims to spend time outside the pods. Some new inductees participate in the feasts and celebrations marking the end of Ramadan only to return to their old routines shortly thereafter. Gang membership is all about "what you can get." Scared Straight programs expose at-risk youth to the realities of prison life. Troubled youth are brought into a special pod for two hours to interact with prisoners, frequently inclined to give youthful offenders the full court press.

"Come here, bitch. You're going to be my bitch."

Several recent studies question the effectiveness of Scared Straight programs to significantly alter behavior. The interstate transfer of prisoners, propelled by the desire of state legislatures to house inmates at the lowest possible cost, produces a number of unintended consequences. Estrangement from family members, particularly wives and children, inevitably leads to a higher divorce rate, as well as a marked increase in violence among these inmates.

By their own authority, AII can transfer inmates to other facilities within the network. Under this scenario, a NA Alaskan inmate gets shipped from an Alaskan facility to one of the corporation's prisons in Arizona. Why? Punishment. Uprooted from everything they identify with, some Alaskans, particularly the Eskimos, simply loose it. At TCF these inmates constitute the walking zombies, continuously medicated, with funds provided through the Alaska State contract.

TCF doesn't allow conjugal visits. This differs from the policy in the Hawaiian prisons.

Inmates must place collect calls to family through a monopoly with one of the major domestic carriers. Rates start at $3.00 a minute for in-state calls, more for long-distance. Few lower-income families can afford a ten to fifteen minute call once a month from an incarcerated family member.

In many jurisdictions, courts now rule favorably on victim's requests for restitution or compensation. Through the process of restitution, the guilty party must repay all monetary gains to the victim. Compensation repays the victim for tangible losses suffered, for instance, damage to property. Funds for court-ordered restitution or compensation can be taken from monies earned by the inmate within the prison, or from funds sent to him by family members. This can effectively discourage family members from helping incarcerated relatives. Few want to work a second job only to see 90% of the money confiscated by the state.

In an effort to reduce tensions within the facility, TCF introduced a canine program several years ago. This first-in-the-nation program was sponsored by a local shelter. Inmates in good behavior cells were responsible for feeding, grooming and training pets who slept within the two-man cell. While successfully reducing violence, the program was disbanded when a CO witnessed a dog licking peanut butter off an inmate's genitals! The "official" story related to shelter personnel was that the dog had bitten an inmate.

The ringmaster of this circus is Warden Cesar Lopez. A big Texan, as wide as a door, the former football player had a reputation for getting the job done. TCF served as the training facility for all of corporate's rising stars from the rank of sergeant on up. Lopez preferentially promoted Hispanics and other minority officers.

Backstopping Lopez are three assistant wardens (AW's)—for Security, Administration (a pencil pusher), and the AW for Programs. The last position was typically a training slot, the new guy used as the warden's hatchet man.

Lopez was called "Papa" by administration secretaries who took turns sitting on his lap.

WORK OR CLASS

TCF wants inmates kept busy. There are essentially two options – work (unless he's wealthy) or class.

Setting the tone for education within the facility is the principal, a position analogous to a high-school principal. Inmate educational records, or SRB's (student record books) are locked in the principal's office, as are all test booklets.

Inmates who acquire a 70% or better on exams are eligible for coveted jobs, particularly in the kitchen, where food is sold through the underground economy. Consequently, test books are like gold.

Principal Dan Tindle is a former drafting teacher with a Masters degree in principalities. A mouse of a man who jumps at loud noises, he keeps staff off balance by pitting teachers against one another.

Within the prison hierarchy (Fig. 1), Tindle reports to Esmeralda Olmos, the Programs Manager, regarded as a stepping-stone to assistant warden.

At TCF, there are five types of classes: religion, life skills, GED, drafting and computer skills. Life skills encompass the soft skills, everything from job applications to understanding the family unit, including such courses as anger management, parenting with dignity and substance abuse. Inmates are eligible to take life skills without a GED.

With the exception of the Alaskans, education is the only time inmates from different states are allowed to mix.

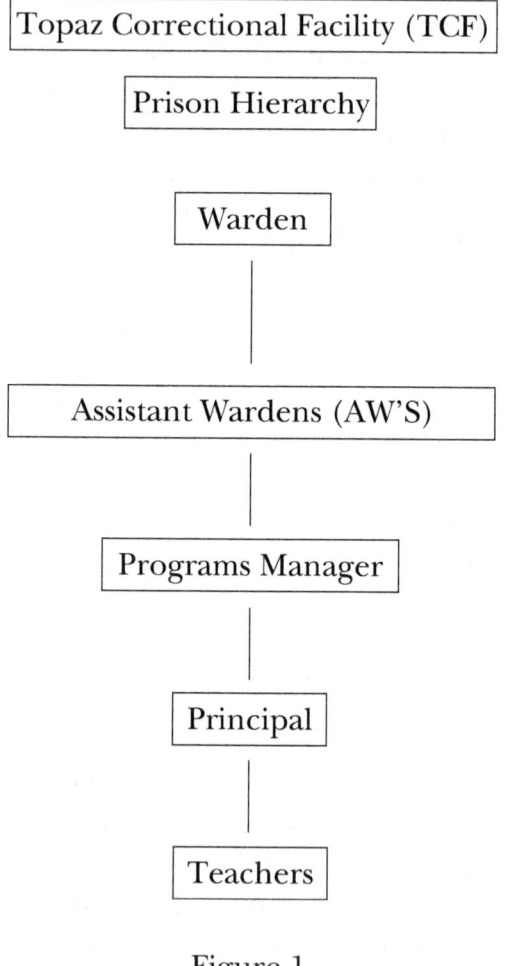

Figure 1

TCF wants inmates in class, not because it values education, but for purely financial reasons. Based on the state contract, the corporation is paid each time an inmate attends class. Teachers are obsessive about "getting the numbers," i.e., filling seats in their classrooms, and are required to file detailed monthly reports on the number of students in their classrooms, how many certificates are issued, and the racial makeup of the class. The stats are collected by inmate-clerks.

Education is incentivized by states housing inmates with private prisons, paying prisoners, on average, eighteen dollars a month to attend classes.

You're probably wondering, "What's the problem?" States pay private prisons to educate inmates, which they do through a well-documented process. The reality is quite different: once inmates sign in, all bets are off.

After sign-in, teachers will accept any excuse to leave. A "dental visit" usually finds the inmate out at the weight stations or socializing in the pods.

While federal guidelines mandate that inmates turn in homework for life skills classes, the mantra of the corporation is "If they show up, just pass 'em."

Critical life skills can only be applied if diligently taught.

"Everyone know what a job application is?"

"Yes."

"Nevermind."

These are life *skills*. You must *teach* them, not simply mention them.

"Once you get on the outside, you have to be able to balance a checkbook."

Education is chronically understaffed. Based on the number of Washington inmates at TCF, the contract between the state and AII requires five teachers. But there's only one. Each state employs a contract monitor to enforce compliance with contracted services. Why isn't the contract enforced?

Aside from espousing a strong anti-inmate bias, "The more you give 'em, the more they're going to want," contract monitors are essentially co-apted by the corporation, provided with an onsite office, company car and subsidized rent. With a secure job, why rock the boat by forcing TCF into spending money for additional teachers? The Washington contract monitor spends a good part of his day watching TV in his office. He can simply ignore inmate requests for additional teachers.

Hoping to ease the excessive downtime in the computer lab, one of the NA Alaskan inmates donated $30,000 to TCF for new computers. Soon thirty new computers arrived. Half were quickly hijacked by administration. Gone were the fifteen-inch flat-screens and CDrom's, replaced by old desktops with floppy drives. The equipment (which was literally purchased at a fire sale) was delivered in singed boxes still reeking of smoke. One third of the "new" computers didn't work. Inmates were admonished to "be careful when you hook 'em up," because some monitors actually blow up. Disheartened, the Alaskan inmate vowed never to donate funds again.

Back home, an inmate earning a GED is a big deal. It's viewed as an important milestone. Within the prison, there are also major ramifications. An inmate can get a better paying job, relieving cash-strapped family members. He's also able to take college courses by correspondence.

From the prison's perspective, it's a losing proposition! An inmate with a GED takes fewer classes, reducing payments to AII! The process is labor intensive, requiring a review of the inmate's SRB, completion of certificates, notification of the state contract monitor, as well as fees associated with administration of the GED by an outside proctor. On the day of the GED, TCF provides one calculator for thirty inmates, when each man actually needs one. Some calculators are broken or mysteriously have no batteries.

There's no incentive on the part of prison personnel to facilitate completion of the GED by an inmate. This explains why so few inmates at TCF acquired their GEDs between 1998 and 2005. Subsequent events would soon cause the numbers to skyrocket, a process fiercely resisted by prison administration.

There are jobs throughout the prison: mopping floors, wiping windows, scrubbing community toilets, and grounds maintenance. Inmates earn from $.25 to $.50 an hour. The kitchen pays the best. Clerks are responsible for computer work, updating files, record keeping, and handling paperwork. Tutors (assistant teachers) who answer questions in class are paid two dollars a day but may get extra compensation to help inmates with their homework in the pods.

Alaskans run the wood shop as part of their state's contract. Using maple wood, they build hobby crafts, toys and clocks that are shipped back home to sell. NA Alaskans carve jewelry, rings and belt buckles from ivory. Positions are awarded by seniority, with a long waiting list. Inmates generally apply when they enter the facility.

CONTRABAND

Within TCF, the Crips and Bloods are primarily involved in the drug trade. The Hawaiians and USO are into loan-sharking, while the Hispanics dabble in both drugs and money lending - stepping on everyone else's toes. Porn is the forte' of the Christian faith pods, facilitating viewing of X-rated material on Gameboys and X-boxes. As TCF is designated a smoke-free environment, cigarettes sell for up to one hundred dollars a pack (no extra charge for state and federal taxes).

Who brings in the cigarettes, drugs, alcohol, porn and meth? Much of the contraband is transported by COs. Employed by a for-profit corporation, they earn less than their counterparts at state and federal prisons, which fuels corruption among the staff.

A drive through the employee parking lot is enlightening. COs own $35,000 pickup trucks, vehicles sporting crew cabs and Eddie Bauer interiors. While state and federal investigators routinely perform credit checks to weed out such corruption, private prisons simply look the other way. Corruption probes bring bad press, adversely impacting the bottom line.

In an attempt to tamp down the transportation of contraband, dogs were placed at the gates during change of shift. Inmates poisoned two of the canines with a mixture of crushed chilis and rat poison.

Searches of the Hawaiian pod rarely turn up banned items. Since their environment is meticulously maintained, they're simply more adept at concealing illicit items. Before fire inspectors caught on, empty fire extinguishers were routinely utilized to store contraband.

As all calls by inmates are taped, the safest way to transact business is to rent a staff member's cell phone. While COs can earn more than a hundred dollars an hour renting their phone, they must carefully consider the downside risk. One morning, at change of shift, an inmate approaches a female CO who's just coming on duty. He lifts his shirt, pulls a cell phone from his pants and lays it on the podium in plain sight of other staff.

He directly addresses the female officer. "Here's your phone."

She's beet red. "That's not my phone!"

The inmate persists. "I paid you $200 to use it."

The previous day, the female CO leased her phone out several hours before end of shift. To recoup his lease fee and turn a profit, the inmate leased the phone to several others and the CO was unable to retrieve the phone before leaving the facility.

That night, with the battery low, another leasee attempted to recharge the phone using a homemade stinger, setting off the fire alarm within the pod.

After the alarm, an investigator conducting a cell search found burn marks radiating from the electrical socket and seared paint on the wall. He ordered the inmate to drop his pants, and observed the antennae from the cell phone protruding from his rectum! The inmate agreed to set up the CO. She should have known something was wrong, since inmates are confined to their cells during change of shift.

The CO was fired. Within the prison, they'd say she was "walked out the front door." No charges were filed. Formal charges attract public scrutiny, highlighting staff corruption at a corporate prison facility.

While the warden and COs are of the opinion that the inmates "are all animals," the nurses love the Hawaiians.

If a nurse is caught going down on an inmate, it's invariably one of the Hawaiians. As usual, no charges are filed. She's simply "walked out."

Within the facility, there are always one or two vacant pods reserved by the COs for orgies.

THE ARRIVAL OF MR G

In April, 2005, Gerard LeMoine entered TCF as a teacher. The son of a white police officer, raised in the projects of New York City, the husky, tenacious ex-marine-turned cop, had come full circle. Now, he was trying to help convicted felons turn their lives around.

Lemoine—known to inmates as Mr. G–was originally hired as the Washington State life skills teacher. Program Manager Olmos wanted him to revamp the curriculum.

"I want you, with all your worldly experience, to run the Life Skills program. See what we have. See what you want to change."

She was referring to Gerard's experience training foreign police officers through a project administered under the auspices of Interpol. LeMoine logged thousands of miles in over thirty-five countries, everywhere from Thailand to Russia, teaching such skills as accident reconstruction, interrogation techniques, the handling of crime scenes, and English as a Second language.

Olmos was explicit.

"Bring us up to twenty-first-century standards. You have carte blanche to do what's necessary. Just run things by us first."

LeMoine nods. Olmos presses the point.

"We want to say in our [AII] sales brochure that we're offering 'cutting edge' inmate education."

LeMoine learned his values from his grandfather, who told him there were three things needed in life to be happy: a sense of honor, a sense of compassion, and a sense of humor.

"If you loose any one of those three, it's time to do something else."

Gerard took those lessons to heart.

"The last thing you want is someone mean and nasty who carries a gun, to deal with a rape victim or exhibits callous behavior at an accident scene."

At a lunch for new teachers catered in the prison library, staff were admonished to keep LeMoine's background confidential. Disclosing such information would place his life in jeopardy.

During orientation, Shirley Borden, an erratic, divorced forty-year old GED teacher, introduces Gerard to a class of Alaskan inmates.

"Mr. Lemoine is a teacher and a former police officer!"

The inmates freak out. LeMoine quickly corrects Borden.

"I'm sorry, guys. What she means is my dad's a retired officer."

Borden interjects, "You told me you were!"

The Alaskans wouldn't hesitate to kill a former cop.

LeMoine scrambles, "No, no, no." He rubs his belly. "Do I look like a police officer?"

The guys laugh, shrug off the gaff by Borden.

In the hallway, LeMoine presses the point. "Don't tell people that!"

She seems to understand. "I'm sorry."

After introducing LeMoine to a second class, Borden closes her remarks—"And Mr. LeMoine is a police officer!"

Gerard takes her aside. "Are you fucking crazy? What part of this don't you understand? You're going to get me killed!"

That afternoon, in a hastily called meeting with Olmos, Gerard expresses his concern.

"This woman's wacky. She keeps telling inmates I'm a police officer!"

"I'll talk to her."

"She's going to get me killed!"

Olmos backs Borden. "You've got a bad attitude! This is a difficult environment for anyone, especially a woman."

She suddenly picks her cell phone off the table, pretending to answer a call, effectively ending the conversation. Bizarre.

Gerard quickly became aware of the free-for-all classroom atmosphere condoned by staff, simultaneously developing profiles on his fellow teachers: Borden's propensity to read romance novels from the top drawer of her desk carried over to her duties as assistant librarian. One of two females authorized to buy books for the prison library, she devoted half the budget to romance novels. This drove inmates crazy!

Tina Villalobos, the head GED teacher, a short, chunky divorcee, spends little time at the blackboard, opting to socialize in the hallway with fawning inmates, while tutors teach her classes. If a dispute breaks out between staff members, odds are Villalobos is in the middle of it. Tutors are frequently targets of Villalobos' vendettas, forced to fend off her attempts to pit them against other teachers.

Villalobos is involved with a NA administrative assistant (slip sliding), who she meets for trysts in the religious storeroom, AKA the Ark, an eight-by-twelve foot closet used to house religious gear and literature.

Phyllis Tubbs, late 60's, reads magazines at her desk, favoring *People* or *Vogue*. A four hundred pound, divorced man-hater, Tubbs previously taught on an Arizona Indian reservation before retiring to the prison.

Tubbs and the other computer teacher, Mr. Chavez, always presided over half-empty classrooms. Mr. G asked inmates what was going on.

"They're not good for their word."

Chavez might promise to bring in a sub sandwich or bacon-double-cheeseburger for whoever got the best grades. He never did. In prison, the only thing inmates have is their word. You can take away their clothes, their toilet paper. They'll sit naked in their cell for days.

"Now what are you going to take from me?"

Their word is most important.

After attending his first staff meeting, Gerard is approached by Olmos and Principal Tindle. Olmos asks how things are going.

"Do you really want to know?"

"Yeah."

"This is a Greek drama, that's turning into a Greek tragedy!"

Tindle holds his head, but LeMoine's just getting started.

"I'm working on my Masters. I'm getting sucked into politics with all these women. I've never seen anything like this before!"

When LeMoine goes for refreshments, Olmos corners Tindle.

"Get him under control. He's coming on like gangbusters, treating me like a cop!"

Every day at work, LeMoine wore a pressed shirt and tie, inadvertently showing up the other teachers. To the COs, Gerard was just the FNG (Frickin' New Guy), but the inmates took notice, as related by one of the administrative secretaries.

"Mr. LeMoine, the inmates respect that."

Then there was the sign above the door in Gerard's classroom:

EDUCATION STARTS HERE. TODAY IS THE
FIRST DAY OF THE REST OF YOUR LIFE.

While the sign suggested a different approach, inmates were unprepared for this new teacher. Classroom exercises became a challenge, forcing them to think for themselves. At first, this made inmates uncomfortable.

"What's the answer?"

"Look it up."

"The other teachers tell us."

"Do I look like them?"

Mr. G had to earn their respect.

"Inmates will lose respect for you if you're easy, if you let them get away with shit. You can be tough, as long as you're consistent and fair, everyone respects that."

Gerard understood that convicts practice the PIG lifestyle–Personal Immediate Gratification: "I want it now. I don't want to work for it. I don't want to save for it." His approach was straightforward.

"I'll do everything in my power to help you help yourself, but you've got to do it."

Inmates in Mr. G's classes were continually asking for the bare essentials, pencils and paper. LeMoine approached Principal Tindle.

"TCF doesn't supply pencils. Here's a box of twenty. When they're gone, they're gone!"

LeMoine started buying supplies with his own funds. At Wal Mart, he purchased pencils and two hundred Meade notebooks. Expenses started mounting. Soon he fell behind in repaying student loans.

In his second month, LeMoine's duties expanded to include assistant librarian, responsible for making legal copies for inmates. A series of lawsuits forced AII to open three law libraries to accommodate inmates from various states researching their cases. During the day, if pulled out as librarian Mr. G had to abandon his classroom.

He caught his first break when he met Roy Gunderson. Just back from knee replacement surgery, the Life Skills teacher was also a Marine, a tough bastard in his early 70's who had been a POW in 'Nam. The inmates respected Gunderson, not for his teaching ability, but because he knew things. He'd been through the meat grinder and survived. Gunderson had also been an assistant warden at one of the federal prisons in D.C. He knew the system, and could point Gerard in the right direction.

Over lunch outside the facility, Gunderson corners Gerard.

"Did Borden invite you home for lunch?"

"No."

"Don't go home with her! She's a nympho. She has sex with inmates in the library and in her office! Best blowjob in the place."

"What's wrong with this woman?"

"Bipolar."

More importantly, Gunderson advises Gerard to acquaint himself with inmates' backgrounds by reviewing their files in the record room.

"I thought we weren't allowed to look at those."

"You'd better look at those!"

From the files, he learns the circumstances resulting in incarceration, previous convictions, number of times in SEG and history of assaults on staff. Of particular interest are threats, intimidation or assaults against the NCO's (Noncorrections Officers Staff)–nurses, secretaries and teachers.

In life skills, Mr. G conducted mock job interviews, as well as teaching inmates to balance a checkbook. He held tie-tying sessions. Lemoine started teaching inmates for obtaining their GEDs. Inmates felt better as their skill-set improved. They didn't feel stupid. As a result, they didn't lash out as much.

Administration asked Mr. G to be the Seg Education Officer.

"Go down there. See if guys sign up for classes."

Down in Seg, Gerard spoke with the inmate in the first cell about signing up for life skills class. The inmate wasn't enthusiastic.

"No, fuck you."

The inmate in the next cell was also disinterested.

"Fuck you. Get out of here!"

Undeterred, he signed three Washington inmates. These guys are more serious about education than the Alaskans or Hawaiians.

On his second Seg visit, Gerard was accompanied by AW Richards, the assistant warden for security/education. Richards walked a fine line between disciplinarian and mentor. On the security side, he ran Seg and Special Operations and Response Team, specializing in the control of violent inmates. But he also handled various education issues. Richards liked to be liked.

One of the inmates who'd cursed at Gerard the week before was now asking for him.

LeMoine was having none of it. "When you start treating me like a human being, I'll return the favor." AW Richards is enjoying the interplay.

One of the Nazis now asks for Gerard.

"Can I get a copy of Mein Kampf?"

Gerard explodes. "No!"

"Fuck you, you fucking asshole. Come in here and I'll kick your ass!"

"I'm coming in that cell. I'm going to kick your ugly, toothless ass!"

LeMoine asks Richards, now up on the second floor, to throw the keys down to him. Richards readily obliges, the heavy key ring making a loud clanking sound as it hits the ground, sliding across the cement floor to Mr. G. Richards wants to see how far LeMoine will take it.

Loud whistling now reverberates throughout Seg, every cell-window slit has a convict's face pressed against it. Half the unit's rooting for LeMoine kicking the convict's ass, half against.

Two COs on the unit yell out betting odds.

As LeMoine opens the cell door, several COs hold him back. The officers then go into the cell to "speak" with the inmate.

By the eighth or ninth trip, three-fourths of the inmates in Seg signed up for classes. Gerard photocopied chapters from the Life Skills text, passing copies to inmates through lunch-tray slots in the heavy steel doors. For an hour over his lunch break, Mr. G went over homework with the guys in Seg.

Subsequently, one of the Aryans in Seg sent out a note to Mr. G:

"I just wanted to write a quick thank you. Not very often do we get people who seem to honestly care about us. I appreciate you going out of your way and looking out for us with books."

While both part of the Marine brotherhood, LeMoine and Gunderson frequently sparred over teaching techniques. To pull inmates into class, Gunderson brought in tapes of the previous week's gladiator matches, aka Ultimate Fighting. Afterwards, guys returning to the pods were all jacked up.

LeMoine couldn't hold back. "For someone who's been around a long time, you're not very smart."

"It keeps 'em in class!"

Inmates were constantly probing, querying Mr. G to see if he really knew his stuff. Consequently, LeMoine did extensive preparation outside the classroom, enabling him to answer any question an inmate might pose. To prepare for a class on job-hunting skills, Gerard collected applications from municipalities and local businesses, including department stores and restaurants. Photocopying the material, he gave every inmate a stack of job applications. The plan was to work on applications for four to five days, then tweak the resume to fit the application.

"This is a job application. Fill it out."

Their response was a mixture of fear and laziness. "No."

As always, Mr. G persisted. "Just do it."

Many simply didn't know how to describe their skills.

"What do we say?"

"What do you do here? Are you a baker, a sous-chef? Put it down."

Later, holding a completed application, guys had a big smile. Inmates handed in three- fourths of the applications. Unbeknownst to LeMoine, they mailed the rest, using TCF's post office box as their return address. While all incoming mail is searched, outgoing mail isn't. Outgoing mail is sealed. Staff merely feel each envelope to insure that weapons aren't transported between facilities.

Several weeks later, four of LeMoine's students received job offers from a local municipality hiring a crew of groundskeepers for its Parks and Recreations Department.

Even Mr. G was surprised. "Jesus, I'm getting $36,000. They're getting 32K to change sprinkler heads for half the year!"

Gerard was tasked to be the Fire Safety Officer for Education, requiring him to inspect roughly a third of the prison, including Education, Seg, nurse's station, library and visitation areas. He reported to the Head Fire Safety Officer, who briefed Gerard:

"Any problems, don't write anything up. We'll have to spend money on it."

"THIS IS OUR
SACRED GROUND"

After several months at TCF, Gerard switched to evenings, 12:30-8:30 p.m., limiting his contact with Tindle, Villalobos, Borden and Tubbs. Working alongside GED/ Life Skills teacher Gregg Lomax, they enjoyed the calm, settled atmosphere on the night shift. Classes were packed, but there was no chaos. All the COs wanted to come down at night to "protect" the two teachers. There was more education at night than at any time during the day.

Gregg Lomax, a former CO at TCF, was an exceptional bull-shitter who had good rapport with inmates and could pull guys into class. A redneck into NASCAR, the former army vet wore a camouflage hat and frequently removed his upper plate, exposing the gap in his top front teeth.

Gerard frequently took Lomax for lunch at a local Mexican cantina or Chinese restaurant. Strapped for cash, Lomax and his wife were caring for his daughter's illegitimate children. A crack addict, the daughter was caught in a downward spiral of drugs and apparently made a living walking the streets. Lomax's only son was killed in a drug-related kidnapping.

Until inmates learned to cope with their personal problems, they'd never be able to sit through classes. Many have Attention Deficit Disorder (ADD). Adapting a technique he learned in the Orient, LeMoine wrote three words on the blackboard:

Focus – Respect – Concentration

"You need to *focus* on the problem you're working on, have *respect* for yourself and each other, and *concentrate*."

Inmates used 3x5 cards to compartmentalize their problems. On the front of the card, they'd write a subject like wife or family. On the flip side, they'd summarize the problem. This taught them to deal with one problem at a time. The cards were rubber banded and kept in their cells. Mr. G needed them to focus on class, leaving their problems outside. After the exercises, everyone started doing their work.

Many inmates looked to Chaplain Proy to address these problems. Much more than a spiritual advisor, Robert Proy often went out on a limb to help inmates. He might arrange security so an inmate could visit a gravesite, or facilitate transfer of an inmate's recently convicted son to TCF.

Ask a teacher the definition of a principal, he might say, "A principal is like a diaper, always on your ass and full of shit." For Gerard, encounters with Tindle were less frequent, but no less stressful.

One afternoon, Tindle announces his intention for teachers to strip search inmates coming into classes from the pods! Included was a cavity search with a flashlight and rubber gloves, a brazen ploy to break the bonds between teachers and inmates.

LeMoine balks.

"You gotta do it!"

LeMoine holds his ground. "Screw it. I'm sick. I'm going home!"

Tindle caves, "OK, take the roster in the hallway."

He hands LeMoine a clipboard telling him to check off inmate's names as they enter Education. While Gunderson also refuses, Lawson, a former CO, has no problem doing the searches. Tindle retreats to his office, shuts the door, pulling the blinds down. A mouse.

Some guys coming into Education get wind of the Brown Spot Inspection (BSI) and hit the bathroom before lining up. Of the 180 inmates searched, nothing is found.

Tindle is soon demoted for incompetence. Once again working as a drafting teacher, he continues fulfilling some of the principal's duties, submitting weekly education reports. For all intents and purposes, the teachers have an acting principal.

If an inmate didn't come to class, Mr. G often followed up. Such was the case with John Silva, a short, musclebound Portuguese inmate, one of the Hawaiian leaders. LeMoine found him in the Hawaiian pod.

"How come you're not in class?'

"You care?'

"Of course I care."

"None of the other teachers care."

"Think I do this for the money?"

Other inmates made fun of Silva because he couldn't read. LeMoine witnessed Silva put on a show for prison staff in the yard, snapping a wooden bat across his chest, after bench-pressing 480 pounds of free weights! Mr. G worked with him. He won Silva over. They became friends. Silva soon signed up for all of Gerard's classes. The word was getting around. You could go to Mr. G. He was a different kind of teacher. At first this confused administration, who thought inmates were talking about Gunderson, also called Mr G. Many inmates called Gerard "Mr. G" because they couldn't pronounce LeMoine.

None of LeMoine's acts of kindness went unnoticed by the wardens, who viewed each one as an act of betrayal.

Academic certificates awarded for completion of classes like anger management, GED and life skills are helpful when coming up for parole. While reviewing inmate's educational records, LeMoine found many were missing certificates and arranged for replacement copies.

Knowing that inmates cherished certificates, but were turned off by the old black-and- white copies with the AII logo, at his own expense, Mr. G designed new color certificates, telling inmates, "You make the effort, I'll make the effort." Inmates now signed up for classes to get a better certificate for their folder.

In class, Mr. G occasionally was forced to reign people in.

"What part of stop clowning around don't you understand?"

This didn't sit well with Steve Kekoa, a 6'4," 300-pound muscular Hawaiian incarcerated for multiple murders. Kekoa uttered something disrespectful to

LeMoine in Hawaiian, prompting John Silva to jump up and confront him. All of 5'6", Silva began poking Kekoa in the chest. "Don't ever disrespect Mr. LeMoine! This is his classroom. Who else gives a shit about us? This is our sacred ground!"

Kekoa spent the next seven days in Seg. The USO turned him in for disrespecting a teacher.

"TOUCH MR. LEMOINE, WE'LL KILL YOU!"

By his seventh month at TCF, between Life Skills, GED, Seg and PC pods, Gerard was teaching 80-100 inmates a day. He picked up the PC pod assignment after requesting permission from Tindle to bring in guest lecturers.

Inmates were bailing out of Villalobos' classes and defecting to LeMoine's. Her tutors found Mr. G's classroom more stimulating. The reason was straightforward: given a choice between learning and discipline or not learning, the inmates wanted to learn. They needed to learn to regain their self-respect.

In addition to his duties as a computer teacher and Warden Lopez's top snitch, Mr. Chavez enrolled inmates in college correspondence courses. Chavez was responsible for submitting copies of inmates' education certificates to the state contract monitor charged with granting permission for inmates to participate in college courses.

While Washington state has a specific list of universities to which inmates can apply, Alaska allows its felons to apply wherever they want. Some schools grant tuition breaks based on GED and test scores.

Unfortunately, Chavez had little fervor for enrolling inmates in college level courses, preferring that they repeat already-completed requirements, thus languishing in the GED program. While he should have been enrolling upwards of twenty inmates a month, in reality, only two or three gained placement. Worse, for those already enrolled, credits frequently went unrecorded because of his failure to properly maintain inmate records. Inmates asked Mr. G to intercede, infuriating Chavez, who informed the warden that Gerard was stepping on his toes!

"I've got sixty-five guys who want to do correspondence!"

LeMoine wasn't going to cover for him. "That's your job!"

At the end of class, Gerard typically collected pens lent out to inmates. This precluded their use as shanks or for tattooing. One day, he was short a pen. LeMoine was growing impatient, but class ended without anyone coughing it up.

Days later, one of the Hawaiians, just out of the hospital, still battered and bruised, placed the missing pen on LeMoine's desk. He'd been beat up by other Hawaiians who knew he'd stolen Mr. G's pen!

It was at this time that the Hawaiians issued a threat to inmates throughout the facility:

"Touch Mr. LeMoine, we'll kill you!"

LeMoine regularly visited inmates in their cells. No other teacher did. He wanted to evaluate their lifestyle, see how clean the environment was. He played to their sense of self-worth.

"Is it appealing to see a clean room or unappealing? If you get some order in your life, especially in a chaotic environment, life is easier, safer. You're opening your perspective."

If a particular inmate were having trouble, Mr. G would go out to the picnic tables in the common area and talk with other guys in the pod.

"Help me help this guy. I'll be back tomorrow. If he resists, let me know. I want this man to reevaluate everything in his life. I know he's better than he thinks he is."

After a while, there was improvement. Inmates liked the improvement.

LeMoine obtained a dual degree in Justice Studies and English as a Bachelor of Interdepartmental Studies (BIS) from Arizona State University (ASU). Through his friendship with Phyllis Lucci, Senior Programs Coordinator for ASU, LeMoine obtained supplies for inmates, provided as a charitable donation by the university.

On his sixth trip back, with a cartload of supplies, he was stopped in the hallway by Warden Lopez.

"Where's that going?'

"Education."

"Push it through administration first."

That was the *quid pro quo*: LeMoine would have to let the corporation skim off the top, but now every inmate in GED had their own Texas Instrument calculator. Through the university, Mr. G procured fifty Hawaiian language dictionaries for his life skills class.

The CO's resented Gerard's rapport with inmates as well as his unfettered access to the pods.

"There's the inmate lover."

"I'm a teacher."

"I HEARD ABOUT THE RUG THING"

Alaskan inmates tell horror stories about the state's parole system. Once back home, former inmates often must travel 150 miles or more to see their parole officer. With no car and limited mass transit, an ex-con stuck in a snowstorm ends up re-imprisoned on a parole violation.

The Hawaiians at TCF fared somewhat better. Captain Linda Alvarez, a senior staff member, served as their cultural liaison, assisting with prison transition. Inmates knew she cared. She'd talk to parole people in Hawaii, attempting to find descent parole officers for guys getting out. Alvarez was also the Hawaiian hearing officer, serving as a mediator between the COs and inmates. Asked by Alvarez for assistance, Gerard sought formal approval from Principal Tindle, responsible for assigning teachers as hearing officers.

"Why don't you have me as a hearing officer?"

"No way!"

No one disrespected Alvarez. She was protected by the Hawaiians. Inmates told Mr. G, "She's getting into trouble [with administration], just like you."

Not quite. As a minority, Alvarez was nearly bulletproof. Borden (handicapped-bipolar), Tubbs (handicapped-morbidly obese) and Gunderson (combat vet) were also preferential hires. AW Richards wanted to boot Borden and Tubbs, but AII was afraid to take action, fearing a discrimination lawsuit. Richards also voiced concern that Alvarez wasn't siding with TCF, and that SORT teams weren't getting as much practice with the Hawaiians.

Back in the classroom, Mr. G's breakthrough came by leveling with inmates, relating to them.

"I've got problems too. How many people want to be here?"

None raised his hand.

"Neither do I. Do I look like a typical teacher who gets summers off? Let's get started and get something done."

In life skills, LeMoine taught by example. When discussing savings accounts, an inmate asked, "How much do you have in your savings account?"

LeMoine was honest.

"I live from paycheck to paycheck. Don't do what I do."

At specified times during the day, Muslim inmates gather in the library, kneeling on their rugs to pray toward Mecca. The prison condoned this practice, denoting the direction of the holy city with a sign on the wall. LeMoine suspected the directions given by administration. Confirming his suspicions with a compass watch, he discovered that inmates had actually been praying toward Reykjavik, Iceland! Shortly thereafter, Mr. G ran into Warden Lopez.

"I heard about the rug thing."

Numerous times during the year, teachers were pulled to do cell searches as two-man teams, an odious assignment Mr. G regarded as a breach of trust between teachers and inmates. LeMoine cut inmates some slack, overlooking soft porn and other minor infractions.

One of the investigators previously employed by TCF was an older, experienced, semi-retired CO who'd carefully go through cells, gently opening inmates personal effects, like radios, with a screwdriver. Birch, the new facility investigator and a brash braggart, broke open radios and TVs with a screwdriver, drawing inmate's ire. When partnered with Birch, LeMoine would remember other duties —"I've got mandatory fire inspection." — and abandon the cell.

TCF tasked teachers for mail searches before holidays and special occasions. Pulled for an early Christmas mailing, LeMoine overlooked naked photos of inmate's wives or girlfriends in Santa outfits. Villalobos routinely tossed them.

"WHAT PART OF 'NO' DON'T YOU UNDERSTAND?"

LeMoine submitted a second request for guest lectures to the warden's secretary, frequently dressed in a sexy business suit, more appropriate for a porn star. He was again rebuffed. When he submitted a third request, the secretary weighed in.

"What part of 'no' don't you understand?"

Gerard attempted to corral Principal Tindle, citing an obscure paragraph from the regs he'd signed when first hired, "Outside guest speakers will be invited to the facility." Now forced to deal with LeMoine's request, Tindle was incredulous.

"Is that really there?"

Fortunately for Gerard, Tindle wasn't very bright. The regs actually designated guest faculty to address prison staff, not inmates! Gerard went to Chaplain Proy. Three days later, the request was approved.

After okaying the lectures series, the wardens quickly struck back: LeMoine was forced to assume duties as the prison's Staff Event Photographer.

Word about the lectures spread quickly. Well over a thousand inmates signed up for the first lecture. Eighty got in.

Warden Lopez cornered Mr. G. "You better control this."

As the first guest lecturer, Mr. G enlisted a pal, Dr. John Birk, a professor of English at a large metro university. Birk devoted his first lecture to a discussion of spiritual channeling, based on a book by his late mother, Marjorie. The response was terrific. Professor Birk subsequently donated several copies of the book to the prison library.

During the first lecture, inmates segregated themselves by gang affiliation, sitting apart from others in the library. LeMoine was intent on shaking things up.

"When you come in here, this is holy ground. Leave that shit out there!"

From then on, everyone sat down together.

"They were relaxed. They talked to each other. Everyone felt good about it," recalls LeMoine.

On his second visit, Birk discussed one of his own books, *Tracing the Round: The Astrological Framework of Moby-Dick*, which unlocks the hidden code of the famous novel by Herman Melville about an adventurous sailor named Ishmael aboard a whaling ship commanded by Captain Ahab. Birk had their attention. The discussion allowed inmates to momentarily escape the bounds of the prison. They asked insightful questions.

Ishmael's sidekick, Queequez, was a Polynisian harpooner who had engaged in cannibalism, a practice Alaskan inmate Kurt Williams asked Birk to expound upon, much to the chagrin of Mr. G., frantically trying to wave Birk off. Williams, a former scoutmaster, was responsible for the murders of numerous boys in his care, whom he subsequently cannibalized. Anxious to leave the restrictive environment of the PC pod, Williams let it be known that he had cancer, but was refusing treatment, a move he thought would placate other inmates. Once inmates caught on to the ruse, he was attacked.

A signup list was established. Admission for all subsequent lectures was on a first- come, first-served basis. At the end of a lecture, many inmates immediately signed up, without prompting.

Returning from lunch one afternoon, LeMoine discovered his catalogue of college courses was missing. One of his clerks had passed the catalogue to leaders of the various gangs, all sitting together in the library writing up a list of courses they wanted taught at TCF! The lecture series had succeeded in bridging the divide between rival gangs. LeMoine was astonished.

On Dr. Birk's second visit, something unexpected happened. Inmates brought their own work for Birk to critique. Birk and LeMoine recruited a mutual friend, Jennifer Green, to join the group.

Together with Green, a high school English teacher, they spawned the idea of publishing a collection of inmate writings–a prison anthology.

LeMoine established strict ground rules for participation in the guest lectures and anthology:

(1) No Seg: Anyone in administrative segregation was dropped from the program.
(2) Inmates must participate in education. This could be any class or structured activity- life skills, GED, typing, even leather shop.
(3) Anyone who misses a class is out of the program.
(4) Every participant in the anthology must type their own material.
(5) Anyone written up for an infraction in the pods is out.

(6) No submissions to the anthology could contain profanity or anti-TCF rants.

Each inmate committed to the program signed an "Educational Code of Conduct" with Mr. G. As usual, LeMoine was blunt and to the point.

"In lectures, you'll be polite, attentive. You'll sit with your hands folded. No starring at the women's tits!"

The publication of Jennifer Green's fantasy adventure, *Jason and the Magic Skipping Stone*, fueled LeMoine's idea for inmates to read books to their children on CDs. That weekend, at the usual meeting between LeMoine, Professor Birk and Jennifer Green at a local coffee house, LeMoine sketched out his idea. CDs attached to the inside cover of the book, along with a note from their daddy or grandfather would be sent for birthdays and holidays. Paid for by funds raised by Mr. G, the project would help repair the bonds severed by prolonged separation from their families.

LeMoine typed the proposal as an official memo on TCF letterhead. Securing signatures from Principal Tindle and AW Richards, he triumphantly presented the memo to Warden Lopez, who was eating a sandwich at his desk.

Lopez was unimpressed.

"Just leave the memo on my desk. Now you may go."

"But Warden, it won't cost you guys a dime! It'll do wonders for inmates' morale!"

Lopez tosses the memo into the "IN BOX" on his desk. "Get out of my office. I don't want to hear anymore about this!"

"But, sir -"

"Out!"

In a subsequent meeting with inmates, including leaders of the associations, LeMoine, Birk and Jennifer Green answered questions related to the publication of the prison anthology. Birk and Green would function as editors.

"Who's going to pay for the publishing?"

Dr. Birk's own firm, Noble Knight Books, would cover publication costs, estimated at two thousand dollars.

"What happens to proceeds from the book?"

Inmates were told their portion of the proceeds would go to charity.

"Yeah us!"

LeMoine cut through the BS in a way that neither Dr. Birk nor Jennifer had license to.

"No, this is bigger than you guys. You're doing this to show the world that you're not a piece of shit, that you're not animals! This is a chance to tell these people, "Don't follow in my footsteps."

A few of the guys were indignant. "What's in it for us?"

Now all three teachers answered, "Your good name. You're making good karma to offset your sins."

The recalcitrant few were quickly silenced by those around them. A collective decision was taken by all in attendance, the USO, Muslims, Aryans, Bloods, Mexican gangs, religious groups and Native Americans to donate net proceeds from the anthology to Toys for Tots.

Contributing to the anthology forced inmates to hone writing and computer skills, while providing an outlet to reflect on past acts, apologize to both victims and family members and educate others about the downside of prison life.

They expressed themselves through personal narratives, poems, short stories, rap lyrics, Bible stories, frequently discussing why they were sent to prison and the personal toll extracted through prolonged incarceration. None denied their crimes.

Jennifer Green explains, "Through the writing, they expressed their emotions and desires."

While LeMoine worked with inmates on a daily basis, Birk and Green typically held lectures once a month, employing innovative techniques to engage inmates.

Professor Birk asked, "What kind of movies do you guys like?"

When they responded, he'd probe further, "Who wrote that?"

Birk continued, "A screenwriter can earn over 200k for a project." Their eyes popped. You could hear a pin drop. Later that evening, inmates signed up for writing classes by the dozens.

Birk brought the script from *Jaws*. Inmates watched the film, while following along with the script. The teachers encouraged inmates to put down comic books in exchange for a book from the prison library, perhaps a Tom Clancy novel.

Jennifer concentrated on creative writing, poetry and short stories, while Professor Birk focused on dramas, novels, screenwriting and personal narratives. The two teachers took turns editing inmate manuscripts. The guys were anxious to receive feedback.

"How can I make this better? What do you think?"

In an unguarded, tranquil classroom, inmates circulated freely, respectful of the teacher's personal space.

"I was not afraid... everyone of them was a murderer," Green said.

Principal Tindle had already denied three requests by LeMoine for the anthology. With things in full swing, Gerard doubled back to cover himself with administration.

Tindle was unyielding. "You'll get your ass fired!"

"You can't keep guys from getting published. They have First Amendment rights. This is part of my educational program. It's within the parameters of teaching them to write."

"Write it up. Submit it."

While the request was eventually approved, as always, there was a price to pay.

Tindle struck back. "Since you've got time for the anthology, you're now the Washington State Education Officer."

LeMoine's additional duties mandated doing monthly reports on all Washington inmates detailing class attendance and certificates issued.

Dr. Birk and several teachers were interviewed for an article in AII's corporate publication touting the success of the guest lecture series. The interview proved to be bittersweet. Mr. G was forced to correct false statements by Gregg Lomax suggesting that Lomax was the driving force behind the educational projects at TCF!

The books donated to the prison library by Professor Birk were quickly stolen. This was a good sign. Inmates took material back to the pods to study!

DETOUR

Inmates, especially those with wives and children, manifest more stress around the holidays. Now, during Easter of 2006, LeMoine was nearing the one-year mark at TCF. Hoping to ease the holiday tension, he purchased thirty-two large chocolate bunnies at a local Wal Mart at an after-Easter sale to distribute to Hawaiians and Washington inmates in his life skills class.

The boss of the Hawaiian clan, an elder in his mid-sixties, heard about the anthology. He stopped in at a GED class. The only Hawaiian present was Iokua, a twenty-five year old gangbanger.

"Where are the others?"

"They're not interested."

The elder spoke with Mr. G about the program.

"I'm going to sign up. I haven't taken a class in twenty tears, but this is worthwhile. I'll bring some guys with me tomorrow."

The next day, the elder returned with over twenty Hawaiians. He told them: If he's going to sign up, they're going to sign up.

"You're all going to read and write."

All the guys signed up for GED classes and life skills.

Under agreements negotiated between AII and various state prison authorities, TCF was contractually obligated to employ twelve teachers: five for the Alaskans, four for Washington inmates, and three to cover the Hawaiian contract. In actuality, there were only seven, forcing staff to scramble whenever there was an unannounced inspection by state education auditors.

This placed LeMoine squarely in the middle of the charade. When the Washington delegation arrived, he was a Washington Life Skills teacher, but was quickly forced to change hats for spot inspections by Alaskan or Hawaiian monitors.

The ruse included changing inmates' diets. On inspection day, good food was rolled out–fresh fruit, fried chicken with mashed potatoes and real butter.

A scratch golfer, Gunderson was dispatched to ferry inspectors away from the facility for tee times and meals at exclusive local clubs.

One morning, the typical monotony was interrupted with a snap inspection by the Washington State Assistant Director of Corrections. As luck would have it, LeMoine's Washington classroom was entirely empty: Mr. G was preoccupied doing fire safety inspections! Gunderson was also off and couldn't be utilized to short circuit inspectors. Gregg Lomax frantically tracked Gerard down.

"We've got a problem. We've got to fill up the classrooms. We have to help Filton!"

Lomax knew he had a tough sell. "How 'bout if we get these guys in there?"

LeMoine was skeptical. "Why?'

"We've got to make them [administration] look good. Filton's in my classroom. He wants to talk to us."

Lamar Filton was the Southwest regional district contract monitor charged with overseeing contract compliance for Washington State inmates at All facilities in

Arizona, Nevada and Colorado. Fond of high-end suits and gaudy gold jewelry, the burly African American rarely left the confines of his cushy TCF office, refusing to provide inmates with basic supplies.

"It's not my job."

Now he needed Gerard's help.

Filton was panicked. "Classroom numbers are down. They [Washington state officials] have given me sixty days to get rosters up. Can you fill up the classrooms with Washington inmates?"

Lomax stared at him. "What's it worth to you?'

"I'll buy you dinner. I'll get you whatever you want!"

LeMoine requested two new computer printers with extra cartridges.

"You got it! You'll have it all by the end of the month."

Lomax and Gerard went to the Washington pod. They told the guys to come down and fill out surveys, promising them they wouldn't miss the basketball game.

By the time Tindle and Filton brought the Washington Commissioner in, both classrooms were packed with red-suited Washington State inmates. Standing room only.

Gerard was teaching out of the Alaskan classroom, the walls adorned with paintings of the Alaskan wilderness, the Alaskan State seal clearly visible. While these were supposed to be Life Skills classes, LeMoine wrote 'Educational Survey' on the whiteboard, his way of sticking it to administration. Tindle not amused, tried to lead the commissioner out.

"Mr. LeMoine is busy right now—"

Washington inmates are supposed to work out of their own classroom. Eyeing the State of Alaska motif, the Washington Program Director pulled Gerard out of class.

"Do you guys share classrooms?"

Gerard changed the subject. "I've got an innovative program I want to talk to you about."

The next day, Gerard filled Gunderson in on what had gone down.

"Why don't we just hire more teachers?"

Gunderson wasn't playing along. "Don't talk about money. TCF will fire your ass!"

"We're in violation of contracts!"

He grabs LeMoine by the shirt and tie. "Don't you dare talk about this in classrooms or anywhere you can be recorded! They'll fire your ass."

Hoping to circumvent a future calamity, Programs Manager Olmos ordered block walls in the classrooms to be whitewashed, removing all murals, a move sure to spark a riot among inmates. Fortunately, her directives were never implemented.

A short time later, a surprise inspection by Alaskan State officials sparked a confrontation between Mr. G and Tindle.

Gerard was uncomfortable fabricating educational activities to cover for the corporation. "If this goes to court, I won't lie."

As far as Tindle was concerned, his professional relationship with Gerard was over. "You're not a team player."

Returning from lunch one afternoon to find his classroom trashed with the remnants of a fundraiser for Black History Month, Gerard was livid. Overhearing LeMoine's rant, Programs Manager Olmos ordered Mr. G and Tindle to haul dozens of boxes of Dunkin' Donuts on palettes up a flight of stairs to the pods.

"Hurry up! If you drop any, you're paying for them!"

Now Gerard was a donut delivery guy. Just another in a long list of indignities.

Carrying six boxes of donuts, barely able to see over the stack, Gerard edged slowly up the stairwell. Tindle, close behind, related his amazement that Olmos had ever hired Gerard, since she hated cops! Olmos' husband was an ex-cop - she'd caught him cheating on her. The donut assignment was payback, to keep LeMoine down.

Suddenly, LeMoine slips on loose Raman noodles, twisting his right knee. Gerard felt a popping sensation as he hit the ground. LeMoine blew out his knee, but Tindle saved the donuts!

At the prison infirmary, LeMoine spoke with the Head Nurse, a female, mid-forties.

"I've got a problem with my knee."

"I don't know if it looks swollen."

"You've got to be shittin' me! It's the size of a softball!"

She walked away.

A male nurse, casually observing the encounter, counseled Gerard. "Yeah, it's fucked up."

"You didn't examine it. How do you know?"

"I saw you limping down the hall!"

He told Gerard the head nurse would try to downplay the incident.

"No one wants to do any paperwork."

He said the head nurse was always angry because she wanted to have an affair with some of the inmates but she was rebuffed because they thought she was unattractive.

The prison was supposed to provide transportation home or to the hospital. They didn't. With an ace wrap and ice bag, Gerard managed to drive himself home.

Later that evening, LeMoine's girlfriend took him to a local hospital. X-rays showed nothing broken. The emergency department gave him a brace and told him to follow up with a family doctor.

Six weeks later, AIG, his insurance carrier, finally granted a request for an MRI.

The orthopedic surgeon said Gerard should be receiving 80% pay on sick leave for a work-related injury, but Gerard was only getting two hundred dollars a week. Fearing he'd be unable to make mortgage payments, LeMoine opted to forgo surgery and, against medical advice, returned to work two weeks early.

On his return to TCF, all of Mr. G's property was gone, boxed up and sent forty miles up the road to the corporation's new satellite prison, TCF2. He'd been transferred.

Without Mr. G, guest lectures at TCF stopped.

Mr. G at his desk, February 2007.

Teachers participate in a Pow Wow in the prison yard:
(left) Kristen LaRue, outreach program coordinator, Joe Jankovsky, Jennifer Green (center), and Professor John Birk (right).

Teachers Kristen LaRue and Greg Holcutt flank Professor Birk.

Phyllis Lucci, Senior Programs Coordinator
for ASU, lectures Alaskan inmates.

Nancy Peterson demonstrates Hook-ups, one of the Brain
Gym®exercises used to diffuse stress.

Green and Birk review inmates' work.

Asian Pacific Islander (API) New Years Celebration, April 2007.

Chaplain Robert Proy at the API celebration.
Proy holds a hand-made pagoda - a momento from inmates.

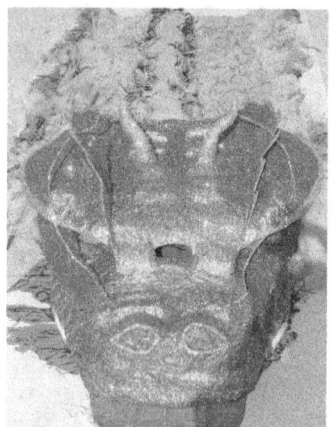

The ceremonial dragon.

Elaborate figures hand-crafted for the
Asian Pacific New Years Celebration.

Ornate artwork designed for the API Celebration

The USO's Code of Conduct.

Native American inmates in elaborate costumes invited to entertain visitors, some coming from as far as China and the Solomon Islands to join incarcerated family members.

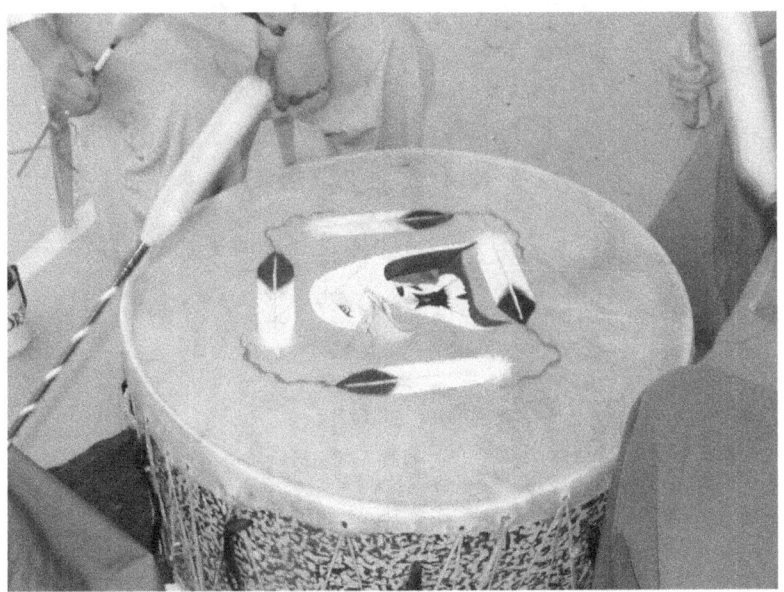

NA ceremonial drum.

Traditional NA arts and crafts presented as gifts to teachers, senior wardens and visiting family members.

Some of the hundreds of egg rolls cooked in the prison yard by African American inmates to afford Asian prisoners more time with visiting family members.

Flag in Mr. G's classroom symbolizes his solidarity with inmates and their desire to attain an education, despite overwhelming opposition by administration.

Joe Jankovsky, Nancy Peterson, Mr. G and Phyllis Lucci.

"THIS IS AN ESTROGEN-RUN FACILITY"

Navigating unmarked corridors within the educational wing of the new Alaskan facility, LeMoine spots the fleeting figure of a woman duck into a doorway. He overhears her say, "If there's no place else to sit, I might as well sit here."

"That sounds like Borden!"

Gerard opens the door to find Borden sitting on a man's lap. As he continues down the corridor, Gerard hears a "bang" as the man tosses Borden off his lap, racing down the hallway after Mr. G. The man catches up to Gerard, nearly knocking him over.

"You must be Mr. LaMonte."

"I'm Mr. LeMoine."

He grabs Gerard's elbow. "Nice to meet you. I'm the Principal, Mr. Boyle."

Boyle is a dead ringer for Fred Gwynne, the character actor best known for playing Dr. Frankenstein's creation, Herman Munster, on the old sitcom, *The Munsters*. Behind his back, staff refer to him as "Frank", while the Alaskans dubbed him "Herman."

Boyle had been an auditor for the corporation, but screwed up, and was busted down to principal. Boyle was so naive, perhaps delusional, he thought it was a promotion! Sure, go out to a facility in the middle of the desert, "It's a promotion!"

Boyle shows Gerard around. The new home for Alaskans and a handful of Hawaiian inmates is woefully understaffed. There are seven COs for four hundred inmates! Boyle warns LeMoine not to discuss staff shortages.

They tour empty classrooms, a library without books, computer rooms without computers. Boyle shrugs, "We've just been taking long lunches every day."

As they chat, Villalobos and Tubbs walk by! They've also been dumped by TCF.

Like a proud father, Boyle asks, "What do you think of this place?"

"I want a transfer. I just left all this back at TCF!"

The teaching staff is in a holding pattern, most pass the time reading or doing crossword puzzles. Vehemently anti-inmate, the Alaskan contract monitor frequently tosses prisoners' paperwork, called "kites," into the trash, "I don't want this crap!"

Confined to the pods for months without TVs, books, or computers, inmates start fighting. Unable to teach life skills or GED without textbooks, Gerard circulates through the pods distributing educational surveys. The surveys determine an inmate's educational level, what classes they've taken, as well as what subjects they're interested in signing up for.

When informed about the surveys, Boyle hits the roof.

"You can't do that! You've got to run it through me first!"

"I did."

"When?"

"Three days ago[never did]. You said it was a great idea."

"OK, have everyone do it."

Borden and Tubbs simply drop surveys on the picnic tables in the pods. No one fills them out. In contrast, Gerard talks to the guys, staying with them while they fill out questionnaires.

Boyle had just asked LeMoine to design a program for Alaskan inmates on small engine repair.

Mr. G asks for clarification. "What type?"

"It's up to you. This is your baby."

Now Gerard has something new to offer. Every guy signs up to learn small engine repair.

The first staff meeting only heightens Gerard's unease. After forty minutes, female staff are discussing their hair and nails. LeMoine reaches the breaking point.

He approaches Boyle. "Can't we get on with this?"

The Vice Principal, Ms. Popovich, weights in. "We heard about you. This is an estrogen-run facility. The sooner you understand this, the better!"

Boyle just smiles.

Afterwards, out in the corridor, the new computers arrive on a push cart. Popovich asks Ms. Navarro to give her a hand in offloading computers. The new education secretary, Navarro was a librarian at TCF but was canned for sleeping with inmates.

Navarro has a better idea. "Get LeMoine to do it. He has descended testicles!"

Popovich finds Mr. G in a nearby classroom.

"LeMoine, pick up the computers!"

"I can't. I'm on light duty. Isn't Ms. Navarro's cha-ching cherry nail polish dry?"

"You've got a bad attitude!"

Popovich slams the door on the way out.

With just two weeks in at the new facility, LeMoine makes the trek back to TCF to talk the warden into giving him his old job back. Several months earlier, Warden Lopez had been transferred to open TCF2, but was never available to interact with teachers, delegating all responsibility to Principal Boyle.

Lopez's replacement at TCF, Warden Sanchez, is a gregarious, self-styled ladies' man with slicked-back hair. Sanchez welcomes Gerard into his office where he holds court with assorted COs and staff. In the midst of a half-dozen hangers-on, LeMoine pleads his case.

Sanchez is delighted. "Here we've got a good teacher requesting to come back. Sure, I'll bring you back. Give me a few days to clear it with Warden Lopez."

Sanchez crows, "This is a dump but they want to work here!"

Back at the new prison, LeMoine designs a top-notch program on small engine repair. The course will offer intensive training in four categories: boat engines, snow-mobiles, motorcycles and chainsaws. LeMoine gathered schematics on engines. He spoke with company reps, securing commitments to send personnel to the prison twice a year, at no expense, to provide certification.

Nearly three months later at TCF2, textbooks finally arrive!

Mr. G presents Boyle with a three-ring binder outlining the entire small engine course for Alaskan inmates.

"That isn't what I want!   I want weed wacker engines!"

"You didn't say anything about that! How many weed wackers do they have in Alaska? Hundreds of Alaskans need jobs!"

At the teacher's meeting, Boyle belittles Gerard.

"Mr. LeMoine doesn't get the concept of small engine repair."

All the women nod in agreement. "We told you."

After the meeting, Boyle approaches Gerard.

"Hey, good news, take the rest of the week off. You're getting transferred back to TCF!"

Boyle tosses the three-ring binder back to Gerard.

"We're getting six weed wackers in next week. My project's going through. Just go. Don't come back!"

"Frank, where'd all the love go?"

THE FALCON AND
THE HITMAN

During LeMoine's absence, Programs Manager Olmos was transferred out after she was caught having sex in one of the cellblocks with the assistant chief of security. With Lemoine back, educational innovation continued. For the first time in months, classes were filled to capacity. There was a 200-man waiting list for Mr. G's classes—another first at TCF.

In GED classes, Mr. G organized tables around individual subjects – English, math, social studies. Gerard assigned tutors to help specific students. No one had ever done this before.

But LeMoine was also tough. "If you don't want to make an effort, drop out. I've got a waiting list."

He also made sure that tutors weren't extorting candy bars or cigarettes for helping inmates with their homework in the pods at night, work they were already compensated for.

Lemoine awarded certificates for perfect attendance, personally covering expenses for the newly designed documents.

Gunderson was annoyed. "Don't do that!"

"With all due respect, your class roster lists thirty guys, but only five are present."

"They get paid whether they're here or not."

The two fought frequently about methods and tactics, Gunderson urging LeMoine to keep a low profile, not to buck the system. He was trying to keep Gerard from getting fired.

Despite their differences, Gunderson managed to scavenge several computers for LeMoine. Subsequently, Mr. G's classroom sported eight PCs, five for GED, three for the prison anthology.

Lon Newman, an MBA-trained inmate, was capable of completing all assigned homework, but was working two prison jobs and was unable to attend classes. Preparing for his parole hearing, he asked Mr. G about awarding him a certificate. Since Gerard couldn't technically give him a perfect attendance certificate, he designed a new certificate for "Outstanding Effort, Homework Only."

Tindle refused to sign it.

"You've got to sign!"

"I can't."

"Sure you can, just go like this." LeMoine took a pen and feigned signing the bottom of the document.

Newman got his certificate.

Meanwhile, work on the anthology continued. Inmates with Masters and Ph.D.s were recruited as tutors, paid out of state contract funds. Each inmate contributing to the project had their own floppy disc, access tightly controlled by 'sign in' and 'sign out' sheets. Chief of Security Pine fought the project every step of the way, forcing LeMoine to turn in frequent logs, while COs performed random checks on discs for escape plans.

Mr. G also engaged in outreach to groups across the prison, arranging for lamb and rice to be delivered to the Muslims for Ramadan. Their own outside religious leader refused to help because the warden was opposed.

The Satanists confronted LeMoine. "What the fuck you doing with them? We don't like those people!"

LeMoine's clerks greased the skids for his numerous duties. Tom Austin, a meticulously organized computer whiz, was a former mob hitman. In and out of the system for more than a quarter century, Austin was never convicted for any of his contract hits! His current stint was as an accessory to murder committed during an armed robbery. On a bank job, one of Austin's inept crew accidentally discharged a firearm, during which a customer suffered a fatal heart attack!

Between jail stints, Austin crashed at his mother's home in Seattle. Well known to local authorities, he worked in the infirmary at the Seattle Zoo. One weekend, Austin brought home an injured falcon. On a long tether, the bird got away from him, gliding into the next yard, swooping down to pick up a teacup poodle. Perched on the adjoining roof, the falcon ripped the flesh off the small dog, as the neighbor lady shrieked in horror.

While awaiting sentencing for the bank job, Austin was visited by two Seattle cops who showed him photos of a local child molester. The perp molested a thirteen-year-old girl from the neighborhood. Austin spoke with the girl's parents. Shortly thereafter, officers revisited Austin. The body of the child molester had just been discovered.

"Know anything about that body that turned up?"
Austin said he didn't.

"Thanks anyway!"

Mr. G brought Joe Jankovsky to TCF. A free-lance photographer and darkroom- exhibition printer, Jankovsky
lectured on digital photography, showing inmates his
personal portfolio. They were excited, several inmates
posing numerous questions on a follow-up visit.

"No one on staff was positive, except for Gerard.
They had a hostile attitude to helping inmates, to
doing anything that could make work for them," recalls
Jankovsky.

Joe subsequently photographed inmates' work for
the anthology.

Five months into his tenure, Warden Sanchez was
fired for sexual harassment. Walked out the front door,
Sanchez waxed eloquently.

"I'll sue your ass! I'll get my Jew attorneys!"

The hallways at TCF began to resemble a university cam-
pus, inmates carrying textbooks and nylon notebooks.
While AII refused to spend a dime above what was specified by state contract, LeMoine frequently went into his
own pocket to cover supplies. It was at this time that
LeMoine was officially notified by the US Department
of Education of the default on his student loans.

When outside lecturers presented, classes ran from
10 a.m. to 5 p.m., each session lasting an hour and a
half. Professor Birk's classes typically attracted over two
hundred inmates.

Another popular lecturer was Nancy Peterson,
brought in by Mr. G to teach inmates Brain Gym.®

Developed over twenty years ago by the Educational Kinesiology Foundation in Ventura, California, Brain Gym is a neurodevelopmental program that helps fill in learning gaps. Increasingly used in the treatment of stroke, autism and Alzheimer's Disease and to help ameliorate symptoms in ADD, hyperactivity and learning disabilities, the technique has been tried in other US prisons.

Brain Gym utilizes a series of repetitive physical exercises to help reprogram the brain, in essence, unblocking cognitive (thought) pathways to facilitate learning.

Inmates were open to Peterson's methods.

"Guys responded big time," recalls LeMoine.

LeMoine's efforts were beginning to pay off. Inmates in the program were working as a community. In classes, former rivals sat together, Nazis alongside Muslims. Their opinions of one another were changing.

"Inside that room was a different ballgame," recalls Jennifer Green.

Egos started to disappear. Inmates got emotional dealing with what happened in their lives.

"All of the sudden, they were in touch with so many things. It was really pretty powerful. They understood what they had done and wanted to turn their lives around," Peterson said.

Of course, nothing's perfect. Acceding to a request by the Muslims to use his classroom for a religious gathering, LeMoine returned to discover they'd ripped a banner off the wall. Created by local high-school students over a week's time, the timeline depicted relevant milestones in US history, including a rendering of noteworthy US Presidents. LeMoine used the timeline to educate Washington inmates.

The Muslims said they couldn't have pictures of idols (Presidents) on the walls.

Mr. G stormed down to the Muslim pod, the 'trouble pod,' pulling the head guy out. Imam Rasheed Said returned to LeMoine's classroom accompanied by two burly guys.

LeMoine showed them the damaged timeline.

Said was upset. "They disrespected you."

LeMoine addressed the bodyguards. "Get out of the room. I want to talk to your guy."

The two left. Now alone with Said, LeMoine didn't hold back.

"No one else gives a shit about you guys. Everyone told me not to do it, that I'll regret it. They were right!"

Said was shaken. Gerard reminded him how he had hooked them up with a butcher for Ramadan. How he'd come into the pods to sign guys up for classes. Now LeMoine wanted the room cleaned up – "Spotless"— and for those responsible to apologize. If these things were done, they could use the classroom in the future.

When Gerard came back from lunch, the classroom was immaculate. Fifty guys were there. Everyone came up and shook his hand as they apologized.

"Any time you want anything, let us know. You can come into the pod anytime."

LeMoine had been warned not to go into the "Black Pod" without a white-shirt (warden or assistant warden) escort. He thought he'd try the Muslims out.

LeMoine walks into the pod. "I need everyone's attention."

One of the brothers responds. "Fuck you! You're one crazy white mother fucker walking in here–"

Immediately the others jumped his case. "You don't disrespect Mr. G. You knock that shit off!"

From then on, LeMoine got nothing but respect, Muslims coming up to him in the hallways, "Good morning, Mr. G."

The simple truth was, the Muslims had no one else. No one else gave a damn about them. For the first time in many months, Gerard felt good: This was a group no one else could deal with.

One day, between classes, Principal Tindle caught up with Birk. After commenting on what a wonderful program the lecture series was, and lauding the educator's plans to publish inmates' work, he finally addressed the central issue.

"Who's getting the money?"

Told that all proceeds after expenses were going to charity, Tindle responds, "If TCF can make any money, let me know."

Warden Sanchez was replaced by Warden Hudsenbeck, previously the AW for administration, a pencil pusher. A devout Mormon, Hudsenbeck was staunchly anti-program. In a meeting with teachers, he laid out his agenda.

"I don't want nothing out of the ordinary. Nothing. The bottom line is what I want— this is reality, folks– we're going to cut staff."

Teachers were told to cut back on everything – printers, ink cartridges, supplies.

An administrative secretary confided to Mr. G. "If it's up to him[Hudsenbeck], we'll eliminate programming. Teachers aren't cost-effective."

Anticipating these draconian budget cuts, LeMoine toiled seven months crafting an educational grant proposal he now submitted to ASU. Mr. G hoped to capitalize on a mammoth $138,000,000 grant given to the university by Phoenix construction titan Ira Fulton.

Fulton's grant stipulated funding for the educationally disadvantaged, an apt description of LeMoine's students. The proposal, for approximately $1.2 million, stipulated roughly $300,000 to cover each of the inmate populations at TCF – the Alaskans, Washington state inmates, Hawaiians and Native Americans. Grant funds would be managed through a nonprofit foundation (501C3), set up by a friend of LeMoine's dedicated to assisting inmates.

Nancy Peterson believed inmates would be better able to process information after doing Brain Gym exercises. Peterson feels the typical inmate tends to be right-brain dominant–i.e., more spontaneous, emotional, living in the moment, easily manipulated–versus the more analytical, detail-oriented left-brain person.

According to Peterson, the left brain allows an individual to more readily process information, to make it his own. If this ability is muted, an individual's actions don't register as readily, and he doesn't fully process the consequences of his behavior. Peterson sought to re-establish left-brain-right brain balance (integration).

Without early nurturing, the emotional part of the brain isn't sufficiently activated. The same can occur with a head injury or lack of bonding. These deficiencies can produce a person devoid of emotion– a sociopath.

"These people were desperate for education. They couldn't thank us enough for coming," Peterson recalls.

Those inmates practicing Brain Gym exuded a calmer demeanor. They began taking an interest in other activities, asking Mr. G to help organize various service organizations, such as The Alaska War Vets and Toastmasters.

As always, LeMoine obliged, "Whatever you do, put your hearts, your souls and your minds into it."

One night, Mr. G, Birk, Green, photographer Joe Jankovsky and TCF Life Skills/GED teacher Gregg Lomax participated in a discussion of inmate education sponsored by a global internet radio station. Listeners around the world queried the five about their experiences. Lomax suddenly began asserting that he had developed the program, forcing Gerard to step in.

"Whoa, it's not your program!"

LeMoine sensed an uneasy vibe from Lomax's wife who had accompanied him to the show.

"In retrospect, this is when things went downhill," says LeMoine.

"WHAT'S IN IT FOR AII?"

Iokua, the Hawaiian gangbanger, excitedly approached Professor Birk.

"Dr. Birk —it's like an atomic bomb went off in here!"

"What do you mean?"

"Ever since we worked on the anthology, there's no fighting!"

The run sheets, the daily roster of all inmates at TCF, confirmed Iokua's claim. Seg numbers plunged from fifty to sixty inmates to just four or five. Attacks on staff were down, as was inmate-on-inmate violence. Library use increased, as did classroom attendance, and the number of inmates acquiring their GEDs.

They knew someone cared about them.

After the three-day July 4th holiday, LeMoine returns only to be greeted by one angry shift supervisor.

"This is all your fault! Look what you've caused!"

She motions toward a metal flatbed pushcart loaded down with large plastic trash bags.

Mr. G is confused. "What is it?

"These are library books!"

LeMoine shrugs. "And, what?"

Her anger rises. "I've spent the entire last two days shaking down the cells and retrieving these books!"

LeMoine's still bewildered by her rant.

"The inmates stole all these books from the library!"

LeMoine breaks into a grin—and is immediately back in the doghouse.

He shakes his head.

"Look —how many fights were there over the holiday?"

"None."

"How many COs got assaulted?"

"None," she concedes.

"How many inmates got stabbed?'

"Okay, none."

"And how was the weekend?"

She nods. "Actually, it was very quiet."

"Okay."

"But this is all your doing, you and your stupid 'anthology project' and other bullshit. It's causing us way too much grief! They mention you a lot in our staff meetings: 'What's LeMoine up to this week'?"

When they reach the library, Mr. G is amazed: The shelves are bare. The inmates had pilfered all the books!

"You'll just use the inmates to fill 'em up again, right?"

The shift supervisor looks at LeMoine.

"Right," she snaps.

The success of the program prompts Dr. Birk to enlist additional outside faculty. He approaches an old friend, Dr. Bob Kaplan about lecturing inmates on screenwriting. Known in LA as "Doc," Kaplan, a former physician, ran an indie production company, Passline Productions. Doc suggests producing a limited series or documentary around the prison program, hoping to foster similar programs nationwide.

With publication of the prison anthology slated for December, 2006, LeMoine begins working on logistics for a graduation ceremony honoring inmates who contributed to the publication. Doc now had two months to write the script, obtain all necessary clearances, assemble a crew and shoot the graduation ceremony, as well as inmate and staff interviews and any additional footage needed for a six-to-seven minute promo based around the anthology, now titled *Voices from the Desert.*

Doc plans to pitch the project at the National Association of Television Program Executives (NATPE), the cable industry's yearly confab held in Las Vegas each January. At NATPE, program executives solicit new content and would be receptive to an edgy project based on a book.

Despite enthusiasm among the inmates, and growing support within the academic community, there was a persistent undercurrent of opposition within the prison. Gunderson typified the views of the anti-anthology chorus, the "no program" crowd, content to "lock 'em in their cells."

What was behind this opposition? The administration was trying to keep inmates down. A surge in inmate self-esteem was threatening to the prison hierarchy. But it ran deeper: the drop in violence produced a domino-effect throughout the facility. There was far less work for the COs, the SWAT team and the infirmary.

LeMoine recalls, "I thought they'd be happy, there were fewer guys in Seg. No, that's how we train our SWAT guys."

The corporation charges double to house inmates in Seg, producing a direct impact on the bottom line.

Now Seg officers were forced to walk the corridors in general population.

Fewer serious inmate injuries resulted in a reduction in ambulance runs to the hospital. Ordinarily, two COs escort an inmate to the hospital. This cut overtime for COs before the Christmas holidays.

With the anthology graduation ceremony tentatively scheduled for Dec. 14, LeMoine organized everything from food to press coverage.

The Hawaiians and Native Americans agreed to perform traditional ceremonial dances dressed in native costumes, following a rendition of Johnny Cash's greatest hits by Vic Fatali. A veteran Cash impersonator, Fatali appears as "The Man in Black" at venues worldwide and arranged to bring his band and a June Carter impersonator. All would donate their services for the event.

Doc partnered with another film company known for shooting high-end commercials. The production now had all necessary equipment, crew, post-production facilities, an experienced director of photography (DP), as well as an additional producer to coordinate the logistics.

Acting as writer and executive producer, Doc ran a draft of the script by Birk, himself an accomplished screenwriter, for a final edit. They depended on Gerard to obtain clearances, but TCF's committment remained far from certain. Suddenly, Mr. G faced a wall of opposition in the form of administrative regulations delivered in a lunch meeting with Acting Programs Director Mullins, the last in a line of individuals hired to replace Programs Manager Olmos. Unlike the others, Mullins came with a distinctive pedigree: Though he perpetually denied it, he was Warden Hudsenbeck's son-in-law.

Mullins was intent on exposing loopholes in Mr. G's proposal.

"What's in it for AII?"

"Free publicity. It's a money-maker. Other states will send [TCF] inmates."

Unswayed, Mullins continues. Now rubbing his fingers together, he again inquires,

"No, what's in it for AII?"

The question already answered, Mr. G remains silent.

"You making money?"

"Not that I know of."

Lunch over, Mullins gets up and walks away.

Later that afternoon, back at TCF, Mullins gives Mr. G a fourteen-page memorandum detailing requirements for the event. TCF was demanding waivers for everything, shunning financial responsibility for any and all eventualities, including, but not limited to, cost overruns due to unexpected pod lockdowns, blackouts from generator malfunctions or electrical storms, inmate riots, fights, infectious diseases obtained from close contact with inmates and theft or damage to production equipment.

Mr. G would have to provide serial numbers for every piece of equipment entering the facility, as well as estimates for additional security personnel and such mundane issues as the number of port-a-potties required.

LeMoine was asked to assemble all information in a standard-operating-procedures (SOP) manual for distribution to wardens, chiefs of security, AII corporate, including the corporation's attorneys —twenty-five binders in all.

The requests were beyond punitive, but Mullins admits as much, "You know, I'm just busting your chops because I have to."

What kept LeMoine going? One night after work, in the employee parking lot, several of the COs wives thanked Gerard for creating a safer environment for their husbands.

To solidify support for the documentary, Mr. G and Chaplain Proy toured the Phoenix production facility. The dog-and-pony show featured a screening of the facility's work, including fund-raising spots for a children's hospital and a woman's shelter. Both ads deeply affected Chaplain Proy, which sealed the deal. While Proy acknowledged the reduction in violence among inmates, as well as an improvement in their appearance and demeanor, he cautioned that the educational program wasn't a panacea. Some 30%-40% of inmates were beyond reach. All in attendance agreed.

Doc and the production team put together letters for AII corporate and the wardens, along with discs featuring the most impactful ads. Soon after, LeMoine was called into Warden Hudsenbeck's office. Hudsenbeck tosses a disc to Gerard.

"What's this?"

"A letter should have come with it. These are the people doing the filming."

Hudsenbeck was turned off. He didn't know how to handle it.

"Did you forward anything to corporate?"

"Yeah."

"When I hear, I'll contact you."

One morning not long after, Gerard was waiting at a crash gate, the barrier between two pods, along with other staff, including a skinny, geeky-looking guy whom he didn't recognize. Suddenly, two inmates walk down the hallway with a large, fourteen-foot wooden ladder and a rope.

"Where are you guys going?" asks Mr. G.

"We're going to do some painting."

"Why don't you have a metal ladder?"

Just then, the gates open. The two inmates go through ahead of LeMoine, who's stopped by the geeky guy.

"What's your problem?"

"Why have a wooden ladder in the prison with an electric fence? They should have metal ladders."

He grabs LeMoine by the belt. "Hey, I'm the new Chief of Security! I bought that ladder. Who are you?"

Gerard doesn't mention his law-enforcement background.

"I'm just a Life Skills teacher."

The chief pokes Gerard in the chest. "Don't worry about it."

"LOMAX JUST STABBED YOU IN THE BACK"

LeMoine sent a steady stream of documents on the anthology graduation to Acting Programs Manager Mullins, but found himself caught in a Catch-22. Without corporate approval, Mr. G was unable to go to the producers for crew names and specific information on equipment required by Mullins.

The ceremony now less than two weeks away, LeMoine stops the warden in the corridor.

"Did we hear anything?"

"Enough of that! Let it be. When I hear, you'll know."

Still without clearances from TCF, Doc's producing partners were growing restless.

The DP felt the production was a bust. "They're backing away."

Ever the realist but hoping to salvage the project, Doc sought to reassure them.

"The warden's behind it. The approval's hung up in corporate."

Coming in as a member of the lecture series, ASU's Senior Program Coordinator, Phyllis Lucci, stressed the importance of learning.

"I spent the entire day at the prison," Lucci recalls. "Every group that I spoke to, the room was jammed."

Lucci sought to emphasize the generic things she'd learned over a lifetime.

"You can loose everything in your life–and I have twice–but you can't loose your education."

Immediately the inmates respected this tough, street-wise Queens-born lady for what she'd accomplished, as well as for her willingness to spend time with them.

With Mr. G and Professor Birk tied up in lectures, Lomax took Jennifer Green, Nancy Peterson and Lucci out to the yard to watch the Hawaiian dancers practice for the anthology graduation.

Lucci recalls, "He thought he was slick. He was trying to pick my brain."

Lomax warns the teachers, "Don't concentrate too much on Mr. LeMoine, he won't be here too much longer. He may be gone by Monday!"

He hands out cards with his contact information. "Go through me."

Later that night, the women briefed Gerard, "Lomax just stabbed you in the back."

The next shoe quickly dropped. Phyllis Lucci received a voicemail from Principal Tindle.

Lucci recalls, "I thought– 'What the hell does this guy want'?"

Phyllis informs Gerard.

"Your buddy left a message on my machine."

"Who's that?"

"Your principal, Tindle. He told me he wants to take over your grant because you don't have time for it."

Gerard confronts Tindle. "What's going on?"

"Are you getting any money out of this?"

"Why?"

"You have a conflict of interest."

"It's none of their [All's] business."

"If you need any help, let me know."

The encroachment by Lomax and Tindle smacked of the interference LeMoine encountered years earlier as a deputy sheriff. Working a crime scene, he was brushed back by two detectives.

"We'll take over."

They handed LeMoine twenty bucks. "Go for coffee and donuts."

As ordered, Gerard bought donuts and a gallon jug of coffee. Outside the store, he stuck his nightstick in a pile of dog shit, stirring it in the jug. Several months later, the same two detectives show up at another of LeMoine's crime scenes.

"Want me to go for coffee?"

"No, that's okay."

Mr. G's anxiety about Tindle and Lomax was temporarily blunted by the delivery of the anthology from the printer. Gerard immediately got copies to Professor Birk, Jennifer, and Doc, as well as the wardens and Chaplain Proy. Ironically, the distribution of the anthology placed Chaplain Proy directly in the warden's crosshairs.

Proy had penned the opening prayer for the anthology, viewed by administration as the ultimate betrayal. Just weeks earlier, Proy had interceded on behalf of NA inmates, compelling TCF to cede land on the yard for a sweat lodge, a revered NA ceremonial enclave. Proy asserted that any NA inmate could participate, while Gunderson argued they had to be 100% Native American. Proy countered that no one was 100%, and succeeded in forcing the permanent land grant, codified in a dedication ceremony attended by outside tribal elders from the Pasqua, Papago and Gila River tribes.

Lemoine met with Proy in the Chaplain's office.

"Word's out. They read the prayer."

"I don't care."

"This is a battle. Your job's on the line. My job's on the line. What do you hear?"

"I haven't heard anything."

Once tight with administration, Proy was now out of the loop.

With just a week to go before the graduation ceremony, LeMoine caught up with the warden in the corridor.

"No word yet?"

"We're not doing it. That's it!"

LeMoine laments, "The less you do as a new warden, the less trouble you get into."

Mr. G was depressed. He thought he'd let the inmates down. Several days later, Gunderson gave Gerard a copy of correspondence he'd lifted from Gregg Lomax's desk. The e-mail, sent by Lomax to the Director of Programs for AII, touted Lomax's development of the guest-lecture series and prison anthology, advising that the program be expanded throughout the system! Lomax closed by requesting more funding for the inmate programs at TCF.

Lomax's request backfired. In the reply e-mail, the Director of Programs responded that he'd never heard of the program and had no intention of funding inmates when outside students have to pay for their own supplies, "We're not giving you a dime!"

Gerard found Lomax in his classroom. Furious, he tossed the e-mail at him.

"We're finished!"

Worse yet, everything was shut down. Everything. There was no graduation. No filming would be allowed within TCF for a documentary.

"Our access evaporated," Doc recalls.

Inexplicably, the guest lecture series was suspended.

"GO FOR IT"

LeMoine was heartened by a stream of inmate donations to the 501C3 to help Dr. Birk defray costs associated with publication of the anthology. Inmates signed "Release of Funds Authorization" enabling TCF to debit their account for the specified amounts. Individual donations ranged from two to twenty dollars. The Alaskans contributed the most money.

More importantly, it was now January, 2007, and Mr. G was still on the payroll. This was no minor accomplishment. Chaplain Proy was recuperating from a heart attack suffered shortly after agreeing to take a suspension. A female teacher accused of bringing contraband into the facility had played on Proy's sympathies. She'd smuggled in a bag of loose-leaf tobacco used by the Native Americans for sweat lodge ceremonies. A half ounce of tobacco can net the smuggler $100! Cornered by investigators, she claimed Proy brought the contraband in!

Teachers can be terminated, Chaplains can't. Knowing the teacher was heavily in debt and was raising several children on her own, Proy agreed to take the fall. He was a chaplain in every sense of the word.

Gerard approached AW Richards, Acting Head of Education, about holding an anthology graduation ceremony. He was hit by a string of No's.

"No security. No family members. No sheet cakes. No graduation! Just go hand them [diplomas]out."

LeMoine didn't back down.

"This is the biggest day in some of these guy's lives! It's the first time they've done something on their own."

On Mr. G's way out, Richards slammed the door behind him. The secretaries recoiled.

AII was under legal assault, the corporation forced to settle two costly racial discrimination suits. Hispanic and African-American COs at two facilities were compensated in a promotions suit. White COs at TCF successfully sued, claiming preferential promotion of Hispanic staff.

Hoping to capitalize on these defeats, Tina Villalobos was now threatening to sue for racial and sexual discrimination! To defuse the situation, Warden Hudsenbeck sent Villalobos to see AW Richards, who promised to act as her protector.

Roy Gunderson summed up the feelings of the staff: "She's untouchable. We're fucked!'"

While talking to a GED proctor at a local community college, Mr. G got wind of a poetry contest for Black History Month. College administrators encouraged LeMoine to enter works by his students. Although the submission deadline was little more than a week away, with backing from Acting Principal Tindle– "Go ahead. They're not going to win anyway"— Mr. G printed flyers.

Ranell Harper and his "nephew" Percy Watkins, both Washington inmates, spied the flyers. Watkins quickly volunteered to distribute the material for Mr. G, who had previously taken Harper under his wing and made him an "unclassified" classroom assistant, a paying position he could never have landed on his own.

Eyeballing his nephew, Harper was skeptical, "Make sure he puts 'em up."

Watkins shot back, "Don't throw your eyes at me."

LeMoine made Watkins give his word that he'd distribute flyers to every pod.

TCF hoped to stop perpetual celebrations by various inmate groups from disrupting the prison routine. Every group from the Wiccans to the Buddhists had their own special events.

One day Gunderson pulled Gerard out of class "to talk." Before LeMoine knew what had hit him, he was standing in Warden Hudsenbeck's office. Attempting to seize the momentum, Gunderson schmoozed the Warden.

"What's with all these celebrations? Who's running this place, us or the inmates?"

TCF would now combine events, which meant delaying celebration of holidays like Black History Month for several months. While Gunderson was trying to buff Gerard's image, Mr. G was now stuck. He would have to delay any further attempt to honor contributors to the anthology.

Mr. G's brother ran a company doing systems design for corporations and universities. Upgrading the network at the University of Nevada, Las Vegas (UNLV), he offered Gerard three hundred used Apple computers, fully a third were laptops with under one hundred hours of use. UNLV would make more money writing off the equipment than reselling it.

Mr. G approached Warden Hudsenbeck, sitting in his office with his feet on the desk tapping a pencil.

"Have I got a deal for you!"

Hudsenbeck holds his head. "What?"

LeMoine explains the UNLV offer.

"What the hell we want that crap for? I don't want that shit! What else you got for me?"

Years earlier, LeMoine worked as a cameraman with Phoenix's Channel 8, the local PBS affiliate. Through his connections, he learned the station was replacing one of their mobile vans.

"We can cannibalize the van and set up a studio in the prison."

"No."

"We don't have to buy wiring, nothing! With equipment, the van is worth $300,000!"

"I don't need any of that shit! What else you want from me?'

"Nothing."

Hudsenbeck stalked out, immediately reaching out to Principal Tindle.

"Rope 'em in."

Tindle caught up with Mr. G.

"All I want you to do is go to your classroom and polish your chair with the seat of your pants! Forget about TV vans and computers. You're a teacher. Don't even do that! Play solitaire on your computer!"

Lemoine was soon teaching again, drawing Tindle's fire.

"What don't you understand?"

"I'm a teacher."

"Just take it easy for a few days."

Shortly after this encounter, Tindle was back working as a drafting teacher. The facility had a new principal, Mr. Sibley. The former Baptist minister knew the system, having worked as a principal at an AII prison in New Mexico.

Sibley approaches Gerard. "We're gonna go for a few beers tonight."

Later, over drinks, Sibley laid it all out.

"I talked to people. Warden Hudsenbeck says you're a pain in the ass, all the stuff you're doing for inmates. He says it's got to stop. These guys [inmates] need people like us. You're causing problems."

"I'm pushing the envelope."

"Go for it."

Like LeMoine, Sibley was a rabble-rouser.

The community college notified LeMoine: One of his guys had won a prize in the Black Poetry Contest. The college asked that he stand in to accept the trophy. At halftime of the girl's basketball semifinals, in front of a packed house, Barrington Campbell, organizer of the contest, announced the second place winner as Percy Watkins–the Washington inmate who'd distributed the flyers!

Mr. G accepted the trophy and a one-hundred-dollar check. He headed for his seat–but was called back up: The first place trophy and two hundred dollars had been won by another Washington inmate.

At TCF for his monthly lectures, Professor Birk acknowledged Percy Watkins.

"Hey Watkins, heard you won the Black Poetry contest."

Uncharacteristically quiet, Watkins crouched down in his seat.

Other inmates spoke up. "What contest? How much you win?'

LeMoine intervenes, "Didn't Watkins tell you?"

"No, Watkins didn't tell us!"

Watkins was quick to cover himself with Mr. G. "Swear to God I put 'em up!"

LeMoine checks the pods himself. Sure enough, the flyers were clearly visible on bulletin boards in the white pods. The Black pods were another story: Flyers were hung up under stairwells, upside down, and buried behind other announcements on the bulletin boards.

Gerard pitched in to help handle an influx of new California (Cali) inmates. By federal law, new arrivals without GEDs have to take a GED placement test within five working days.

This directive didn't sit well with Clive Bacon. Covered with tats, the burly gangbanger in his mid-forties was doing time for the murder of a store clerk during an armed robbery.

LeMoine recalls, "If you ran into him in a police uniform, you'd have to shoot this guy. They don't pay me to bleed."

Called out of the pod with other inmates for the test, Bacon dissed LeMoine before the whole class.

"I don't need to take the test–motherfucker!"

"If you don't take the test, we're going to put your ass in Seg. It's up to you."

LeMoine took the time to explain the situation to Bacon.

"All you need is one math test, and you get your GED..."

He showed Bacon his computer printout.

"... and the highest of all your scores was in math!

Bacon got teary-eyed. Now he was mad as hell.

"For three fucking years my wife's been working a second job so I can get an extra dollar a day."

The state of California never told Bacon he needed only one class for his GED. Had he known, he could have secured a better-paying job, alleviating the pressure on his wife.

LeMoine recalls, "He went from an aggressive ass-hole to a pussycat."

"Do you want help from me or not?"

"Yes, I'm sorry."

"The guy's whole life just unfolded in front of him," Gerard says.

Later that day, out in the yard, Bacon spoke to the Washington Imam through the fence.

Bacon was told that LeMoine was untouchable from every standpoint.

"We can't afford to lose him. No one else gives a shit!"

Bacon put the word out to his Cali buddies: Everyone would cover LeMoine's ass.

Once again, Mr. G was stretched too thin. No one was doing their job. Gerard was only supposed to be on loan to California. Now, in addition to doing Washington state paperwork, he was doing stacks of California documentation!

LeMoine approaches Villalobos. As Head GED teacher, this was her responsibility.

"Why am I doing this?"

As usual, she was indignant.

"If you keep this up [helping inmates obtain their GED], you'll have over one hundred guys graduate! A lot are only one or two classes short! I don't have time to track them down."

Villalobos was responsible for reviewing inmate SRB's (student record books). While she signed off on reviewing files, when Mr. G questioned individual inmates, she never spoke with them! This was a violation of American Correctional Association (ACA) policy, which mandates review of inmates' GED files.

What was the protocol at TCF? It was for teachers to brow-beat inmates into retaking unnecessary courses.

LeMoine was getting nowhere. He approaches Gunderson.

"Outside these walls, you have people depending on these guys to get their GEDs."

Gunderson was unmoved. "Don't worry about it. Fuck 'em. We can't save the whole world."

On the morning shift there was always a wait entering TCF, as COs checked ID's. Proper procedure was to physically touch the ID with the forefinger, while examining the photo.

LeMoine noticed COs physically touch each ID without looking at the picture!

Mr. G decided to test the system. Obtaining a set of 'floating eyeballs' used on toys in the woodworking shop, he slipped a pair onto his ID photo.

After a few weeks without a single comment from the COs, he clued Gunderson in.

"How long have you had that?"

"Four weeks."

"Your shittin' me!"

How was LeMoine caught? By the COs? No. The inmates picked up on it while waiting with Mr. G at the crash gate. A CO happened to overhear them talking and reported back to the geeky Director of Security, who reproached Gerard.

"That's not funny! Take those off!"

"OUTSIDE! OUTSIDE!"

In early March, Elizabeth McNeil, Director of Undergraduate Academic Services for the Department of English at a large metro university, accompanied Professor Birk on a visit to TCF. A staunch advocate of prison education, McNeal spearheaded an effort to distribute over 7000 texts and CDs to a number of prisons throughout the US.

During the tour, which included informal meetings with Wardens Hudsenbeck and Richards and Georgette Foulston, an attorney with AII corporate, McNeal offered to donate textbooks, including audiobooks and books in Spanish.

TCF officials assured McNeal that they were open to additional lectures by university faculty and welcomed a visit by William Mawin for Black History Month. A former Sudanese child-soldier, one of the Lost Boys of Sudan, Mawin, a galvanizing public speaker, often brings audiences to tears as he describes the plight of child-slaves in his nation.

The anthology graduation ceremony at TCF was moved from the library to a classroom to accomodate a larger gathering. As the ceremony took place, each contributing inmate received a book and a certificate as a "Published Author" or "Published Artist'". Special certificates for "Outstanding Effort" were awarded to those inmates who crossed gang lines to help others read and write so they could contribute to the anthology.

Handing out books and certificates, Mr. G shook each inmate's hand.

"Congratulations, you're a published author."

As Mr. G greeted each contributor, the room burst into spontaneous applause.

Inmates went around signing each others' books, requesting signatures from Jennifer Green, Professor Birk and Mr. G. The depth of emotion was unexpected, many Native American and Asian inmates crying on receipt of their certificates.

Inmate after inmate thanked Mr. G for pushing them, driving them further than any had ever dreamed of, toward a goal many thought was unattainable.

Iokua, the Hawaiian gangbanger, immediately sent his copy of the anthology to his parents. In the midst of a religious conversion, he had translated the Lord's Prayer into Hawaiian as his contribution to the anthology.

Professor Birk approached Stark, one of the inmate-authors, in for narcotics and auto theft.

"Mr. Stark, congratulations! You did a great job!"

Turning away, crying, Stark responded, "You know, this is the first time that anyone's given a shit about what I've done in my life. I really want to thank you, Mr. Gerard."

The other guys were dead silent.

Professor Birk broke the awkward silence. "Use it as a starting point."

The Imam and the Asian leader were emotional. They spoke in front of Wardens Hudsenbeck and Richards.

"We've been locked up for many years. You're the first teachers who cared. Thank you for spending your time to help us. You helped tear down the walls."

The next day, Mr. G, Birk and Jennifer went to TCF2 to award certificates to Alaskans and a handful of Hawaiian inmates for their contribution to the anthology.

Arriving at the facility, the teachers spot some of their guys doing grounds work. As their vehicle passes the second barrier, one of the inmates glances at the car.

"Professor Birk!"

Birk calls out to him, "We're here for the anthology!"

Word gets out, "They're here!"

Some of the inmates inside the fence are now running alongside the car!

The teachers enter the classroom, Mr. G transporting boxes of books on a pushcart.

Gerard opens one of the boxes. "Gentlemen, this is your work."

A large cheer erupts from the forty-odd inmates assembled in the classroom.

Warden Lopez refused to attend. Prior to the ceremony, many of the inmates were rounded up and placed in a pod next to Seg.

"They wouldn't tell us what was going on. We thought we were going to Seg. We've been here for hours!"

With his name attached to a $1.2 million grant proposal, it was only a matter of time before LeMoine received a visit from AII corporate. Summoned to the principal's office, Mr. G was met by three attorneys, two men and a woman. Georgette Foulston, the same attorney who'd met with Liz McNeal, wants to speak with him.

"What do you want to talk to me about?'

"Let's talk outside."

Afraid to be recorded, she refuses to engage LeMoine in conversation within the facility.

"Outside, outside."

They walk through three crash gates, two electric gates and two outside fences. Foulston walks LeMoine out to the far parking lot, where rapes occur.

"Unfortunately, the way you've got it [the grant] written, you want to control this money.

That's unacceptable. How much money are you making on this?"

"None of your business."

"If you get any money, it has to go to corporate."

"I get to spend the money any way I want to spend it."

"No! It has to go through committee. They'll be six or seven people who all have to be compensated. What's the money for?"

"Paper, books, supplies, video. Anything we need."

"Totally unacceptable."

"You can't stop it. You're not going to get any money. I'm going to control it."

After such a rousing vote of confidence from corporate, the high point of LeMoine's week came in a phone call with William Mawin, one of the Lost Boys of Sudan. His arrival highly anticipated by the Muslims, Mawin offers LeMoine a sense of what he hopes to impart to inmates.

"You've got to make better decisions with your life. People are dying to come here. You have the greatest opportunity in the world."

WALKED OUT

While proctoring a testing session for new Cali arrivals, LeMoine observes an inmate slip out of class carrying a TABE (Test of Adult Basic Education) test booklet. Mr. G chases the inmate through two sets of crash gates. Pulling him aside, he checks the inmate's folder, now empty.

"What'd you do with it?'

"It's gone."

He had handed off the booklet to one of his Cali buddies in the hallway.

"Why'd you steal it?'

The inmate said he needed the money.

"You put me in a bad position."

The inmate's laughing.

"Don't you know you're going to Seg?"

"I don't care."

With a test booklet, inmates can readily secure correct answers from a college-educated prisoner, rendering testing meaningless.

Of significance, the missing test booklet was a Level Eight–inmates working in the kitchen are required to have an eighth-grade education. A kitchen assignment gives an inmate a significant bump in daily pay from $1.00 to $1.60.

Facility Investigator Birch was notified. After conferring with administration, the warden ordered the entire education department for California shut down until the booklet was found.

Principal Sibley immediately suspended ABE (Adult Basic Education)/GED classes until the booklet could be recovered. The California pod was locked down for cell searches.

Unable to locate the missing booklet, the COs give Mr. G their take.

"We can't find it, so you miscounted!"

Birch approaches LeMoine. "You're costing us a lot of money." He winks at Mr. G.

"Did you miscount?"

"I didn't miscount the books."

LeMoine recalls, "I could see the tape recorder in his pocket. He didn't even put black tape over it–I could see the red light through his shirt!"

Every day education is shut down AII looses thousands of dollars. The California program was shuttered for five days. The corporation desperately wanted to retain its California contract, the largest state contract ever signed by AII.

Warden Hudsenbeck held an educational meeting. He stressed AII's rising share price, encouraging teachers to "BUY, BUY, BUY!" He reiterated the gravity of the situation.

"There's an escape clause in the [California] contract that states if we fail to provide x number of days of education per year, they have the right to terminate the contract."

Suddenly, the impasse is resolved: Gunderson, in charge of keeping records, declares all books accounted for.

Birch relays the news to LeMoine. "Gunderson swears they're all accounted for."

"Did you go down personally and count them?"

"No."

His credibility now on the line, Mr. G enumerates numerous flaws in the handling of test materials by the education staff.

"We found one [test booklet] on a table in the PC pod. Borden left it there. We've found booklets in inmate's cells during cell searches. If you check Villalobos' desk you'll find some.

"That's not necessary."

In a followup memorandum to Birch, LeMoine recounts these incidents, including one in October 2006, when he discovered TABE test booklets bearing the TCF-AII stamp for sale in a local bookstore. The clerk described buying them from a woman fitting Villalobos' description! She was looting material from the education storeroom to supplement her income.

LeMoine repurchased eight booklets with his own funds. Returning the materials to the prison, he informed Acting Principal Tindle, who instructed LeMoine to put the booklets on his desk.

Hudsenbeck tells the assembled teachers he's being forced by corporate to restart classes, AII enforcing its edict by threatening Christmas bonuses. Every teacher now turns and looks at Mr. G.

LeMoine shrugs. "The Calis have us over a financial barrel."

Hudsenbeck smiles. "Let's go to class!"

Classes soon resume for Cali inmates, without Birch locating the missing test booklet. Above all else, AII wanted the money—so much so they broke their own cardinal rule, "Theft of educational materials will result in suspension of classes until such 'restricted items' are recovered."

Cali inmates now had the upper hand. If faced with losing revenue, AII would kowtow to their demands. If push came to shove, all inmates had to do was boycott classes.

In early June, as promised, Liz McNeil returned to TCF with ten boxes of books. This time the reception wasn't as welcoming.

"They were definitely not thrilled to see me," recalls McNeil.

LeMoine receives a call from security, "This lady's mad. They [administration] won't let her in."

Mr. G meets with Wardens Hudsenbeck and Richards. He reminds them of McNeil's previous visit with Dr. Birk.

"You shook their hands. You said 'We love this, bring them in.' "

"Enough is enough!"

"Well, she's here. What do you want to do?"

"We'll take the books."

"This is the woman you said could bring the Lost Boy in."

"No Lost Boy!"

Out in the parking lot, Liz McNeil unloads the car herself. Gerard comes out with a push cart.

"Warden Hudsenbeck just denied you permission to come in."

McNeil had never been turned away from a facility before. She was angered by the abrupt about-face.

"They promised me in the hallway. They shook my hand. They don't want this program to work!"

Several days later, LeMoine received notification that his $1.2 million grant proposal could not be reviewed due to ongoing litigation. The university was being sued by the Fulton Foundation for failure to distribute the endowment as specified by Ira Fulton. Apparently, ASU's intent was to distribute the interest on the $138 million, not the money itself. Any leverage LeMoine had with TCF was now gone.

That Friday, TCF held a graduation ceremony for Washington inmates. LeMoine's involvement as a GED teacher was a game changer for the prison. In six months, Gerard helped more inmates obtain GEDs than had earned them in the previous six years! In the process, he alienated half the teaching staff, shown up for their lack of initiative, and provoked the ire of administration. Mr. G attended the ceremony– as Staff Event Photographer.

Addressing the graduates, Principal Sibley stuck it to the wardens.

"Don't let anyone tell you if you have a GED you can't go anywhere. I want you to understand, you guys wouldn't be here now if it wasn't for Mr. LeMoine and Mr. Gunderson."

Villalobos wasn't mentioned. She quickly left the event. Sibley continued,

"You guys learned to focus when you have discipline. Carry this with you for the rest of your life. Mr. LeMoine taught you guys discipline and self respect. He did everything asked of him."

Sibley wasn't finished. It was now obvious he was looking at Gerard, seated front row center.

"I want you to know how much you meant to us. You'll always be valued. I want you to know, in my heart, you're the best of the best."

The following week, Sibley altered the schedule, diverting Gerard from teaching to in-service training. This was odd, since LeMoine wasn't up for training for four more months. Sibley didn't tell Gerard what was going on, but he didn't look well.

On Wednesday, over the lunch hour, Mr. G was pulled out of in-service training by the new AW for Education. Coincidentally, Sibley, Warden Hudsenbeck and AW Richards were away.

Over a meeting in the warden's office, recorded by an administration secretary, the new AW laid it all out.

"We have to let you go! Here's your paperwork."

"I could lose my house! You've got to be shittin' me!"

"What part of 'we have to let you go' don't you understand?"

"The whole thing!"

Gerard scans the paperwork, listing numerous "infractions," including loss of possible contracts with the State of California, embarrassment to AII, and "unprofessional behavior".

"You're terminated for bringing in contraband."

"What contraband?"

"TABE test booklets!"

"That was a year ago!"

"I'm new here."

"You've got to be shittin' me!"

Now the secretary is laughing.

"What did you say?"

"What part of 'you've got to be shittin' me' don't you understand?"

The AW addresses the secretary.

"Don't write any of this down."

She leaves the office. He hands LeMoine a copy of the termination notice to sign. TCF had forced Sibley to issue the order of termination.

The AW points to the signature line with his pen.

"Just sign here. You going to appeal?"

"Yeah. I've done more for these inmates than anyone."

The AW points his finger at Mr. G.

"I know."

"You're firing me for bringing in TABE test booklets that we can't photocopy and the corporation is too cheap to buy?"

"You're out of here."

As LeMoine leaves the warden's office, he's escorted to his locker by Facility Investigator Birch. They walk down the center of the hallway, past inmates along both sides of the walkway, to the refrain of COs intermittently yelling,

"Up against the wall!"

Birch, fearing a riot, counsels LeMoine. "Don't say nothing to these guys. Now's not the time."

They walk past inmates lined up in the hallway, over one hundred guys lined up for special lunches, Muslim Kosher lunches, "Pill-Call."

Birch continues to banter with LeMoine as inmates call out to Mr. G.

"You did good for these guys."

"Hey, Mr. LeMoine. How you doin'? You don't look so good."

"How's the anthology going?"

Gerard is taking it all in, as Birch continues.

"You going to appeal this?'

"You're damn straight. Why didn't they give me an option to resign?"

"We don't do that."

In the teacher's storage room, a converted classroom, as Gerard empties the contents of three lockers into banker's boxes, he finds two TABE test booklets.

He asks Birch, "How could the count be accurate?"

"I know nothing about that."

"Don't you understand what this means? These TABE test booklets are supposed to be locked up."

Then LeMoine finds two more booklets.

"Aren't you going to bring these up to show the new AW?"

"No, I'll get them later."

"You showed me your official report. You wrote that every one of these TABE booklets was accounted for. You said none was missing."

Birch just stares at him.

"You going to do a follow up investigation?'

"No need. Just pack your shit. You're out of here!"

LeMoine made three trips to his car. Then he returned to drop off his badge, signing a waiver that he was leaving the facility in good condition.

Walking back outside, the gate closing behind him, Gerard hears a thumping sound, someone banging on a thick glass window! Turning, he sees an inmate looking out at him from a window in the Visitor's Center.

Word was spreading quickly through TCF: Mr. G had been walked out.

The inmate's outstretched hand was pressed against the tinted glass, a furtive attempt to connect with Mr. G. The man, dressed in a red jumpsuit, was from Washington State, though Gerard was unable to discern his identity.

Telegraphing his frustration, LeMoine puts his hands on his hips, looking down at the ground as he shakes his head. As Gerard drove out of the lot, the inmate's hand was still pressed against the window. LeMoine lowers the driver's window, waving goodbye.

"LET'S DANCE"

Gerard pounded the pavement for six weeks but was unable to secure employment. The job market was closed to LeMoine. He'd been blackballed by AII.

Laid-off workers are eligible for unemployment benefits, but those who've been terminated are not. Undeterred, Gerard applied for unemployment benefits through the state's Department of Economic Security (DES), filing a formal appeal on the basis of wrongful termination.

A week later, LeMoine receives a call from DES. A staffer performing a review of LeMoine's appeal conducts a taped interview. For thirty minutes, Gerard lays it all out, from his background, to the TABE test book fiasco, giving Sibley and Gunderson as references.

"You've got solid grounds. I'll get back to you in a week."

Since TCF failed to respond to repeated queries from DES, LeMoine was awarded unemployment benefits of one hundred eighty dollars every two weeks for four months.

Subsequently AII appealed the decision. Gerard won the appeal, but was then sued by AII in an action filed with the state's Superior Court. Filed on behalf of AII by Georgette Foulston– the attorney from the parking lot — the suit claimed Gerard had injured the corporation's good name and demanded reimbursement of unemployment benefits! Any time an AII employee collects unemployment, the corporation's contribution to the state unemployment-compensation fund rises. Thus it's cheaper to fire personnel than to lay them off.

Personnel in the courthouse clued Gerard in. "You're one of the first ones [AII employees] to get unemployment!"

"What can I do?"

"If you take this to court, anything you say in court, any evidence you submit during your wrongful termination/unemployment hearing can be used in a wrongful termination civil lawsuit against the corporation."

Court employees advised LeMoine to submit a detailed list of everything he planned to submit as evidence and wished to discuss during the trial.

LeMoine sent Georgette Foulston a three-page memo listing point-by-point all the dirt he'd unearthed from day one until the day he was fired. He noted in closing:

"If you want to dance, let's dance."

Two days later, a process server for the Superior Court knocks on LeMoine's door.

"AII's dropping the case against you."

Along with the documentation, Georgette Foulston penned a message on a post-it note,

"Have a nice life."

After learning of Mr. G's forced departure, many inmates refused to attend classes. Prison officials responded by scattering contributors to the anthology to corporate facilities around the country. TCF soon instituted a program for inmates to read books to their children on CDs, the very project conceived by LeMoine that they had refused to consider. Now there was a twist: AII applied for, and received $1.2 million in government funding. As well, money voluntarily debited from inmate accounts to defray costs of publishing the prison anthology were never released by the prison.

After decades behind bars, the Hawaiian elder was paroled. Back on the islands a short time, local authorities receive a call: A crazy man was waving a gun. When police respond to the location, the elder bursts from his house, guns blazing– and is shot dead: suicide by cop. After so many years in the system, without mainstreaming by the facility, he was unable to cope with life on the outside.

Weeks after LeMoine's departure, several inmates escaped over the fence–with a wooden ladder.

PRISON TRANSITION PROGRAMS

Transition programs facilitate the assimilation of inmates back into society. An effective program helps inmates avoid the many pitfalls awaiting them by providing a comprehensive safety net— i.e., food, housing, job training, employment, transportation, medical care, including substance abuse counseling, and spiritual/ moral support.

What happens at TCF? On his release date, the inmate's driven into a large metropolitan area by van, often late at night, and dropped on a street corner with a stipend of one to two hundred dollars.

"You're free to go."

The inmate lucky enough to have a relative or friend in town gets a warm bed for the night or for a few days. What if the relationship suddenly sours? The ex-offender is back on the street. How long will it be before he's rearrested?

Aside from education and job training, successful transition requires a high level of organizational support. Inmates need extensive preparation behind the walls, intensive one-on-one. What type of problems did they leave behind? What does he expect to find when he returns home? How does he behave at a jobsite? An ex-offender has to prove himself daily. Uniforms must be clean and ironed. He shouldn't show up on time but early, working twice as hard as his co-workers. He needs to be respectful, "Yes ma'am. Yes, sir."

This begs the obvious question: If we currently spend $60 billion a year simply housing inmates, what's the cost associated with the programs we're recommending– $100 billion a year? With exploding state and federal deficits, who's going to pay the tab?

But costs cut both ways. Successfully transitioning inmates will save tens of billions of dollars a year by breaking the cycle of perpetual incarceration, what New York Mayor Michael Bloomberg calls "turnstile justice."

As you'll see, many of the most successful transition programs are grassroots (often faith-based) efforts or are public-private partnerships.

A pilot program within Arizona's prison system illustrates the kind of public-private partnerships necessary to foster successful inmate transition. A group of selected inmates within the minimum-security facility receive intensive training in job-interview techniques from the local branch of a national internet search engine. There are classes in green construction, carpentry and welding, courtesy of an internationally recognized construction company.

Religious groups provide evening classes in life skills, stressing attire and manners. Farmers contiguous to the prison provide land, enabling inmates to grow their own food. "Inmate Navigators" from a local college coordinate accommodations for newly released inmates.

The fierce dedication necessary to repair shattered lives is amply demonstrated by theses novel transition programs:

The Lovelady Center
7916 2nd Ave. South
Birmingham, AL 35206
(607) 539-1143

The Lovelady Center (TLC) provides a path from prison or domestic abuse to self-sufficiency for women in the state of Alabama. Housed in a 288,000-square-foot facility originally built as a hospital, the faith-based, non-profit transitional community was founded in 2004 by former real estate developer Brenda Spahn.

At that time, women released from Alabama prisons were given ten dollars and a one-way bus ticket back to the county where they were convicted. Teaching Bible studies to female inmates, Spahn was determined to impact the state's high recidivism rate. Ms. Spahn initially housed released inmates at her seven thousand square foot estate, subsequently purchasing the hospital property.

According to Director of Development Vernetta Young, 86% of women complete the highly structured program consisting of both classes and counseling, within six to nine months.

Following orientation, Loveladies attend life skills classes for twelve weeks, including parenting, anger management, substance abuse and domestic violence courses. Community members are randomly drug-screened.

TLC addresses every facet of these ladies' lives, rebuilding dignity through both spiritual renewal and such services as an in-house beauty salon.

Job readiness classes teach resume' and interviewing basics, while GED and vocational training is provided in partnership with Jefferson State Community College, faculty teaching on-site at TLC.

TLC's Personnel Division offers area employers both temp-to-hire and direct-hire options for graduates of the program, all bondable through the Federal Bonding Program. Aside from driving members to and from the worksite, TLC provides daycare as a state-certified daycare facility and home schooling, instruction provided by Freedom Rain Christian Academy.

On a typical day, TLC houses close to three hundred women and over a hundred children. The annual budget is approximately $2.6 million.

Funded by church, corporate and individual donors, The Lovelady Center currently receives neither state nor federal funding on a consistent basis.

Exodus Transitional Community, Inc.
161 E. 104th Street
New York, NY 10029
(917) 492-0990

Exodus, a Harlem-based transitional community highlighted during President George W. Bush's 2004 State of the Union speech, is run by Executive Director Julio Medina.

Medina, who says he "went from dealing drugs to saving lives," experienced a gradual spiritual awakening while in some of New York's toughest maximum-security prisons, earning a Masters of Divinity while at Sing Sing. Three years after his release in 1996, he opened Exodus, helping over 3,000 men and women with the re-entry process during the past decade. Espousing the philosophy "There's no such thing as throw away people," this faith-based model relies on the Exodus Contract. Geared toward helping individuals achieve reintegration into society, the six-page document focuses on six interconnected areas–employment, education, family, spirituality, health/physical fitness and community service. Each participant is assigned a contract coach.

Exodus provides job-readiness training through resume prep, critiques of videotaped mock interviews, computer literacy, life coaching and job placement, guaranteeing every participant at least one interview.

Hoping to stem the tide of imprisonment of inner-city youth, Exodus mentors the children of inmates. Statistics show nearly 70% of these children will eventually be incarcerated themselves.

Many of those working within the Exodus community were formerly incarcerated, all vowing to insure that "No one goes back."

Exodus has an established donor base consisting of a network of upper-echelon churches within the African-American community of New York City, as well as corporate and governmental funding, including the departments of Health and Human Services, Justice and Labor.

Focus Group Prison Ministries
6300 Deane Hill Drive
Knoxville, TN 37919
(865) 694-3837

The tremendous financial burden imposed by the burgeoning prison population is readily illustrated in the state of Tennessee, where costs to house inmates top $438 million a year. Founded in 1992, Focus (Follow Our Choices Unto Success) Prison Ministries is a highly structured, faith-based program providing full-coverage transitional support. The program's vision statement encapsulates its philosophy, "Transformation, not rehabilitation, by focusing on Jesus Christ equals true freedom."

To ready inmates for release, a dedicated group of volunteers, in conjunction with Focus Christian Academy, provide one-on-one work in the maximum security units, offering discipleship and life skills classes, weekly support group meetings, evangelistic events and transition counseling.

Participants develop a life-plan centered on short and long-term goals, including GED, vocational training and college courses. Focus' Family Support Team provides transportation to prison for family members on special occasions. Other team members work with at-risk youth, sponsoring weekend events and mentoring the children of inmates.

Once released, Christian ex-offenders who have faithfully participated in the program are eligible for post-release services. This six-month program, sponsored as a joint venture between Focus Ministries, Peace At Last Ministries and the Knoxville Leadership Foundation, provides food, housing, clothing, as well as spiritual, financial and substance-abuse counseling. Successful transition necessitates job-readiness training– i.e., job assessment testing, resume prep, and interview training. Apprenticeships are arranged with local businesses through the Christian Ex-Offender's Services (CEO's) Program.

Transportation is available to participants via volunteer drivers, bus passes and the Wheels for Success program, providing donated used vehicles for individuals with a permanent job, valid driver's license and insurance coverage.

Focus' Christ-centered holistic approach results in a recidivism (re-incarceration rate) rate of less than 20%– compared to the national average of 68%.

While education and job training are critical, for many individuals, the third essential element is spirituality, accounting for the preponderance of faith-based organizations among the more successful grassroots transition programs.

Two of the more innovative state-run transition programs originate within the California penal system:

California Prison Authority (CALPIA)
Marine Technology Training Center

The Marine Technology Training Center's prison diving program at Chino's California Institute for Men

(CIM) trains one hundred participating inmates a year for lucrative, but dangerous underwater jobs. Initiated in 1970, the one-of-a-kind program was terminated by budget cuts in 2003, but subsequently reinstituted by CALPIA in an attempt to dent California's daunting 70% recidivism rate.

During the rigorous eleven-month course, participants log 2000 hours of academic and physical work, including a requisite five-mile swim, to become eligible for certification from the Association of Diving Contractors International.

Upon release, graduates are capable of numerous difficult and dangerous tasks, including underwater welding and repair work and jobs as commercial or deep-sea divers. Many are able to secure six figure salaries.

The return on investment is well worth the effort. Training costs per inmate run $3,500 a year—compared to the $47,000 price tag of housing an inmate in California. Only 6% of graduates are subsequently rearrested.

California Prison Industry Authority (CALPIA) Carpentry Apprenticeship Program

In 2006, CALPIA instituted a first-in-the-nation, carpentry-apprenticeship program for female inmates at Chino's California Institute for Women, modeled on the successful program for males at California State Prison, Sacramento. Women acquire the skills necessary to apply for jobs in the construction trades, learning everything from concrete pouring and framing to installing roofing. Paroled graduates get a year's paid union dues and a fully loaded tool belt.

The re-assimilation of incarcerated war veterans (Vets) is a vexing problem:

Incarcerated Veterans Transition Program (IVTP)
Homeless Veterans Reintegration Program (HVRP)
Volunteers of America
1134 Lexington Rd.
Louisville, KY 40204
(502) 636-0771

On any given night, over 150,000 homeless veterans live on our nation's streets. In the latest year for which data are available, the Bureau of Justice Statistics estimates 140,000 Vets were incarcerated in prisons across the U.S.

In 2004 the Department of Labor (DOL) established the Incarcerated Veterans Transition Program (IVTP) as a pilot project in six cities to care for veteran ex-offenders at risk for homelessness. The Louisville hub operates under the auspices of Volunteers of America, a nationwide nonprofit founded in 1896. Keith Hammond has worked as an outreach worker for IVTP in Louisville and described the typical protocol used with incarcerated veterans.

IVTP outreach workers regularly visited Kentucky prisons, seeking eligible Vets who were six months from release, for completion of GED and substance abuse programs (SAP). Workers then located suitable apartments, paying one to two months rent, before meeting the released inmate at the prison gate.

Immediately upon release, Vets were typically taken for a meal at a fast food restaurant (their request), before stopping at a bank to cash their release check. Men were then outfitted with civilian clothes, bedding, and pots and pans purchased from Wal Mart and other local outlets.

In Kentucky, any money in an inmate's wallet upon his admission goes to the victim's compensation fund. The wallet and all contents are subsequently shredded. Consequently, team members routinely obtain separation documents (DD214s) for released Vets, to establish identification. Paroled veterans were driven to the Circuit Clerk to obtain a Kentucky ID card, enabling ex-offenders to obtain a driver's license and replacement Social-Security card.

The released offender typically leaves state prison with a thirty-day supply of all meds, dispensed on blister packs. However, private prisons discharge inmates with whatever's left on the blister pack, forcing personnel to quickly set up each Vet with a VA doctor to insure a continuous supply of medication.

Although IVTP met its objectives, successfully stabilizing released Vets, the program was phased out on June 30, 2007. Nonprofits now garner 20% of the funding previously received from DOL. No money is available for apartments. Now a program manager for the Louisville branch of the Homeless Veterans Reintegration Program (HVRP), Hammond laments this shift in focus. Released Vets now live in shelters, having hit bottom, before HVRP kicks in to assist them. HVRP is more jobs-driven. Team members locate homeless Vets, preparing them to go back to work in ninety days. The program provides ID services, work clothing and bus transfers.

When available, housing is provided through a patch-work of government programs, including VA Grant Per Diem, HUD's Shelter Plus Care Program and HUD VASH (Veteran's Affairs Supportive Housing). The VA grant-per-diem program is available to eligible honor-ably discharged Vets for one-to-three years, paying facilities a daily rate to house individuals.

New Directions
11303 Wilshire Blvd., Bldg. 116
Los Angeles, CA 90073
(310) 914-4045

Helping to feed, clothe and house formerly incarcerated veterans, New Directions is a remarkable organization. Housed in two buildings on the grounds of the West Los Angeles VA Hospital, the nonprofit (501C3) provides on-site housing for over one hundred fifty Vets, living in two-person rooms.

The kitchen serves three meals daily, while a mix of paid and volunteer staff provides remedial education, helping Vets obtain GEDs. Life-Skills, computer courses and video-assisted training in job interview skills are also provided.

An outreach team from New Directions scours jails, nearby prisons and LA's skid row. The facility maintains its own substance-abuse recovery program. "They're literally transformed," says full-time staffer Matt Davison of residents in the New Directions program. Chairman of the Incarcerated Veterans Committee of VietVetNow, Davison recently transported nine residents by van for a tour of the West Basin Waste Water Facility in El Segundo, California, as New Directions was applying for grant funds to train Vets in green industries.

The organization receives some funding through the Homeless Veterans Reintegration Program (HVRP), but is heavily dependent on donations.

THE PRISON ANTHOLOGY: *VOICES FROM THE DESERT*

The anthology's utility as a portal into learning far exceeded Mr. G's expectations. Aside from developing writing and computer skills, the project gave participants a sense of purpose, as well as a newfound ability to cope with incarceration and the separation from families and society.

Through the writing, the men were able to open up to their loved ones in a way not possible before. More than one inmate said the anthology saved his marriage. Many expressed a sense of accomplishment never before realized.

"For the first time in my life, my wife and child say they're proud of me."

Reading each other's work, the walls between members of various gangs receded. Contributors came to realize that they shared the same hopes, desires and fears.

"I'm just like you."

The anthology provides an intimate window into each inmate's thought process. Its individual works run the gamut of emotions from despair to rage, sorrow to hope. From the works submitted, Professor Birk identified six distinct themes:

(1) memories
(2) coping (inmates embracing what Birk calls the magic bullet for success - education)

(3) ethnicity and identity

(4) fantasy

(5) love   (inmates demonstrating a profound concern for the lack of love in their lives)

(6) faith (the recognition that life's journey includes
the embrace of a higher power)

The profound impact of education is perhaps best
expressed by Bruce L. Bennett in his anthology entry
entitled "Reading With Humanity," an eloquent testi-
monial to the meaning of education to his life, his very
existence. Here are some excerpts:

"Just as the campaigns of Napolean gave us the Ro-
setta Stone, my incarceration gave me the library, thus
enabling me to discover and translate the treasures of
my own soul, giving me meaning and inspiring me to
look again at the sky above."

"To me, the library represents life itself: every book
is a heartbeat, every page a blood cell, every syllable an
atom of oxygen. To the prison population (it is my be-
lief) the library is a door to hope, without which the
Department of Corrections may very well become the
Department of Abandonment, thereby perpetuating an
already too high rate of recidivism. The library is Mercy,
a beacon for the lost, a place where the lonely and mis-
guided might find an icon of humanity toward which to
aspire. I in fact, assert that the library is humanity, our
endeavoring record of collective consciousness."

Currently out of print, *Voices From The Desert* may be
republished as an e-book through Noble Knight Books.

EPILOGUE

Over the past two decades, the trend toward privatization of prison facilities has only fostered growth of the industry without tangible reform of the system.

Let's be clear: We're not advocating early release or leniency in sentencing - you do the crime, you do the time. Nor do we suggest that all inmates can be rehabilitated. Clearly some 30%-40% within the system, including sexual predators, can't.

By and large, most prisons say it's not their job to train or educate inmates.

Whose job is it?

How was LeMoine able to reduce violence and increase self-esteem among so many hard-core offenders? Mr. G provided an aggressive educational program, coupled with motivation. Most importantly, he *changed inmates' world view.* For the first time, many saw themselves and others as *human beings worthy of love.* They regained their self-respect, their self worth.

As eloquently noted in the treatise "Reentry and Prison Work Programs" written by Shawn Bushway in 2003, "The success of work programs to reduce recidivism depends on whether prison management ultimately buys into the goal of successful reentry." Clearly, the administration at TCF does not. Wardens within the private prison system regard education and training as non-cost-effective. This is the crux of the problem. Private prison corporations, beholden to shareholders, only show a profit by keeping the facility operating optimally, at full capacity.

Within the private prison industry, there is an intense drive to continually build more facilities, as well as to directly influence lawmakers to provide a steady flow of new inmates through the passage of mandatory minimum sentencing and Three Strikes laws. Such a mindset led to the recent scandal in Pennsylvania, where two judges were sentenced to lengthy prison terms for railroading over a thousand teens into juvenile detention facilities run by a private corporation, in return for millions of dollars in compensation!

While the government has shown a willingness to intervene in the day-to-day business of corporations (witness the banking, insurance and auto sectors), ongoing government contracts with private-prison firms facilitate the means to change the system nationwide. Government at all levels–federal, state and local, must forge public-private partnerships between educators, employers, faith-based organizations and prisons to successfully reintegrate the great majority of these individuals back into society.

AUTHORS' NOTE

This story is based on real events. For reasons of privacy and legality, all prison and staff names have been changed.

GLOSSARY

AII - Advanced Inmate Incarceration - US corporation running dozens of private prison facilities.

AW - Assistant Warden

Cali - In the context of this book, the term refers to a California inmate.

CO - Corrections Officer

Compensation - court-ordered repayment by an offender to a victim covering economic losses like property damage.

Contract Monitor - Individual working for a state (Alaska, Hawaii), whose job is to monitor the prison corporation's compliance with that state's contract provisions.

Gangbanger - a member of a gang.

NA - Native American

PC - Protective Custody - Snitches (informants) and child molesters are placed in PC for their own protection.

Restitution - Court-ordered repayment of all monetary gains to the victim by the offender.

SEG - Administrative Segregation - Inmates who are violent, mentally unstable, or facing punishment for specific infractions are sent to SEG.

SRB - Student Record Book - Contains all the inmate's educational records, including certificates and test scores.

Suicide by Cop - The act of committing suicide by drawing a weapon or firing on police, compelling them to shoot in self-defense.

TCF - Topaz Correctional Facility - private prison in the desert SW owned by Advanced Inmate Incarceration (AII).

REFERENCES

Aizenman, N.C. "New High In U.S. Prison Numbers." *Washington Post.* 29 Feb 2009. 30 Jul 2009: 1-3. www. washingtonpost.com.

"Assistance for Homeless Veterans." Volunteers of America. 3 Oct 2009. <voa.org>.

Austin, Paige. "Diving for Hope." *PE.com.* 2 Dec 2006. Dec 5, 2006. www.pe.com.

—. "Governor congratulates carpentry program grads at prison." *PE.com.* 7 Mar 2008. 2 Jul 2009. www.pe.com.

Bennett, Bruce L. "Reading with Humanity." Excerpt from *Voices from the Desert,* ed. John F. Birk. Instant Publishing, 2006: 93-94.

"Beyond the Walls." Focus Prison Ministries. 11 Jun 209. <focusprisonministries.com>.

Bushway, Shawn. "Reentry and Prison Work Programs." Urban Institute Reentry Roundtable:Employment Dimensions of Reentry: Understanding the Nexus between Prisoner Reentry and Work. 19-20 May, 203: 1-17.

"Career Technical-Education-Carpentry." CALPIA. 2 Jul 2009. www.pia.ca.gov.

"Christian Transition Program." Focus Prison Ministries. 4 Sep 2008. www.focusprisonministries.com.

Cook, Pamela. "Ex-con helps ex-cons transition and transcend." *Spirituality.com.* 11 Jun 2009. www.spirituality,.com.

Hensley, J.J. "Private-prison plan raises concerns." *Arizona Republic.* 14 Jun 2009: B3.

Hewitt, Bill. "Young Lives Ruined." *People.* 13 Apr 2009: 60-63.

"Incarcerated Veterans Transition Program." Veterans' Employment and Training Service. Washington, D.C.: U.S. Dept. of Labor, n.d.

Johnson, Kevin. "Calif. diving program helps anchor ex-inmates." *USATODAY.com.* 11 Jun 2009. <usatoday.printthis.clickability.com>.

The Lovelady Center. 24 Jun 2009. <lovelady.homestead.com>.

"Marine Technology Training Center." CALPIA. 2 Jul 2009. www.pia.ca.gov.

Medina, Julio. "Embracing the Journey." Exodus Transitional Community, Inc. 11 Jun 2009. www.embracingthejourney.com.

Noonan, Margaret E., and Christopher J. Mumola. "Veterans in State and Federal Prisons, 2004." *Bureau of Justice Statistics: Special Report.* May, 2007: 1-16.

"Pa. youths want tainted convictions tossed." AT & T (AP). 17 Jul 2009. <my.att.net/scripts>.

Schembri, Anthony J. "Scared Straight Programs: Jail and Detention Tours." Florida Dept. of Juvenile Justice, n.d.: 1-15.

Silverstein, Ken. "US: America's Private Gulag." Corp-Watch. *Prison Legal News.* 1 Jun 2000. 29 Apr 2009. www.corpwatch.org.

"A Unique Approach to Reentry." Exodus Transitional Community. 11 Jun 2009. <wwwetcny.org>.

"U.S. Prison Population." Law & Econ Prof Blog. 24 Apr 2009. <lawprofessors.typepad.com>.

INDEX